W9-DEW-863

KAFKA

KAFKA

•

Ritchie Robertson

A BRIEF
INSIGHT

STERLING

New York / London
www.sterlingpublishing.com

STERLING and the distinctive Sterling logo are registered trademarks of
Sterling Publishing Co., Inc.

Library of Congress Cataloging-in-Publication Data Available

10 9 8 7 6 5 4 3 2 1

Published by Sterling Publishing Co., Inc.
387 Park Avenue South, New York, NY 10016

Published by arrangement with Oxford University Press, Inc.

© 2004 by Ritchie Robertson
Illustrated edition published in 2010 by Sterling Publishing Co., Inc.
Additional text © 2010 Sterling Publishing Co., Inc.

Distributed in Canada by Sterling Publishing
$^c/o$ Canadian Manda Group, 165 Dufferin Street
Toronto, Ontario, Canada M6K 3H6

Book design: The DesignWorks Group

Please see picture credits on page 167 for image copyright information.

Printed in China
All rights reserved

Sterling ISBN 978-1-4027-7530-7

For information about custom editions, special sales, premium and
corporate purchases, please contact Sterling Special Sales
Department at 800-805-5489 or specialsales@sterlingpublishing.com.

Frontispiece: Franz Kafka in 1906.

CONTENTS

•

ACKNOWLEDGMENTS

•

I AM VERY GRATEFUL to Nicholas Murray, for letting me read his new biography on Kafka in manuscript while working on this book, and to Tony Phelan (Keble College, Oxford) for reading my own manuscript and making generous and incisive comments.

Some passages are adapted from "Kafka as anti-Christian: 'Das Urteil,' 'Die Verwandlung' and the aphorisms," in James Rolleston (ed.), *A Companion to the Works of Franz Kafka* (Rochester, NY: Camden House, 2002), pp. 101–22, and from "Scandinavian modernism and the battle of the sexes: Strindberg, Kafka and The Castle," the Spring 2003 Rodig Maxwell Lecture, published by the Department of German Studies, Rutgers University. I am grateful to Camden House and Rutgers University for permission to reuse them.

Ich schreibe das ganz bestimmt aus Verzweiflung über meinen Körper und über die Zukunft mit diesem Körper

Wenn sich die Verzweiflung so bestimmt so an ihren Gegenstand gebunden ist, so zurückgehalten wie von einem Soldaten, der den Rückzug deckt und sich dafür zerreißen läßt, dann ist es nicht die richtige Verzweiflung. Die richtige Verzweiflung hat ihr Ziel gleich und immer überholt (Bei diesem Zeichen zeigte es sich, daß nur der erste Satz richtig war

ONE

Life and Myth

●

THE BARE FACTS of Franz Kafka's life seem ordinary, even banal. He was born on July 3, 1883, in Prague, where his parents, Hermann and Julie Kafka, kept a small shop selling fancy goods, umbrellas, and the like. He was the eldest of six children, including two brothers who died in infancy and three sisters who all outlived him. He studied law at university and after a year of practice started work, first for his local branch of an insurance firm based in Trieste, then after a year for the state-run Workers' Accident Insurance Institute, where his job was not only to handle claims for injury at work but to forestall such accidents by visiting factories and examining their equipment and their safety precautions. In his spare time he was writing prose sketches and stories, which were published in magazines and as small books, beginning with *Meditation* in 1912.

Much of what is known of Kafka has been gleaned from the massive amount of notebooks and diaries he left behind. A page from one of his diaries is shown here.

In August 1912 he met Felice Bauer, four years his junior, who was visiting from Berlin, where she worked in a firm making office equipment. Their relationship, including two engagements, was carried on largely by letter (they met only on seventeen occasions, far the longest being a ten-day stay in a hotel in July 1916) and finally ended when in August 1917 Kafka had a hemorrhage which proved tubercular; he had to convalesce in the country, uncertain how much longer he could expect to live. Thereafter brief returns to work alternated with stays in sanatoria until he took early retirement in 1922. In 1919 he was briefly engaged to Julie Wohryzek, a twenty-eight-year-old clerk, but that relationship dissolved after Kafka met the married Milena Polak (née Jesenská), a spirited journalist, unhappy with her neglectful husband, who translated some of Kafka's work into Czech. As Milena lived in Vienna, their meetings were few, and the relationship ended early in 1921. Two years later Kafka at last left Prague and settled in Berlin with Dora Diamant, a young woman who had broken away from her ultra-orthodox Jewish family in Poland. However, Kafka's health declined so sharply that after moving through several clinics and sanatoria around Vienna, he died on June 3, 1924. During his lifetime he published seven small books, but he left three unfinished novels and a huge mass of notebooks and diaries, which we possess only because his friend Max Brod ignored Kafka's instructions to burn them.

It is from these materials that Kafka the cultural icon has somehow been constructed. This mythic Kafka is typified by the morbid recluse in Peter Capaldi's short film *Franz Kafka's It's a Wonderful Life* (1994). After struggling to write the first line of *The Transformation*, this "Mr K" is eventually drawn into Christmas festivities and unbends enough to say "Call me F." The tormented Kafka is for the twentieth (and so far the twenty-first) century what the somber figure of Byron was for the nineteenth.

Kafkaesque is as potent an adjective as *Byronic* used to be. But while the image of Byron was that of a sinister and sexy aristocrat scorning social and religious taboos, the image of Kafka, by contrast, is a democratic one. The very mundanity of his biography confirms that Kafka was one of us: rooted in ordinary life, he experienced or imagined ordinary fear, distress, frustration, to an extent that we can all empathize with because it corresponds, if not to our actual experience, then to our apprehensions, even our nightmares.

Kafka at the age of five.

The myth of Kafka, like the myth of Byron, was founded by the author himself. It is based, if not in the author's experience, then in the way he shaped and elaborated that experience in thinking and writing about it, first for his own and then for the public's consumption. In both cases, the author himself is hard to distinguish from his fictional self-projections. Byron's readers imagined the man himself as being as disillusioned and gloomy as his heroes Childe Harold and Manfred. It is equally difficult to separate Kafka from the protagonists of his novels, whose names are progressively reduced (Karl Rossmann, Josef K., and the mere K. of *The Castle*). Kafka himself encountered this difficulty. In January 1922, checking in at a mountain hotel, he found that the staff had misread his booking and written his name down as "Josef K[afka]." "Shall I set them right or shall I let them set me right?" he asked his diary.

Since Kafka the cultural icon is ultimately of Kafka's own making, there is no way of going back beyond it to unearth the real Kafka. The anxious diarist and the author of interminable, often agonized and agonizing letters to Felice Bauer and Milena Jesenská are as much the real Kafka as the highly competent professional man, the keen amateur sportsman, and the novelist who did occasionally lose himself blissfully in successful writing. The point is not to correct the iconic image of Kafka, but to go back to Kafka's own writings and see how he made his experience, and the circumstances of his life, into this image. At the same time, there are many factual errors about Kafka in circulation, some going back to the distortions of early biographers and memoirists, and these can be amended by suggesting an accurate and rounded picture of his life and its historical setting. But let us begin with Kafka himself.

Kafka was a very self-analytic, sometimes a self-obsessed, writer. His diaries and letters contain many reflections on his own life and how it has gone wrong. His fictional writing was a less direct way of shaping and comprehending his experience. On October 15, 1914, after taking a break from work to concentrate on *The Trial*, he records: "A fortnight's good work, partially complete [!] understanding of my situation." Although innumerable threads connect his experience and his fiction, and there is some value in identifying them, his work cannot, any more than that of other writers, be reduced to its presumable biographical origin. It is because his fiction so infinitely outgrows its occasions that Kafka compels our attention.

The "Letter to His Father"

To gain some sense of Kafka's own experience, and to see how he began fictionalizing it in the process of reflecting on it, let us look at his longest piece of self-analysis, the famous "Letter to His Father." Kafka wrote this letter, analyzing his relationship with his father, in November 1919. He seems to have intended to send it to his father in the hope that it would clear the air between them, but his sister Ottla, to whom he showed it, and his mother, to whom he apparently gave it first, dissuaded him, and he kept it as a personal document, which he could show in 1920 to Milena in order to help her understand him.

The letter is first and foremost an attempt at self-therapy. Kafka is trying to make sense of his relationship with his father as a means of distancing himself from his father. Since it serves a purpose in Kafka's own development, we must not take it as a balanced or complete portrait of Hermann Kafka. Nevertheless, there is no reason to suppose that anything in the letter is actually false, and it presents a plausible picture of a powerful personality. Hermann Kafka was a self-made man, brought up in the southern Bohemian village of Osek in extreme poverty. At the age of seven he had to wheel a peddler's barrow through the villages. These youthful hardships were such a vivid memory that he used to bore his children by constantly recounting them and complaining that the young generation did not realize how well off they were. By incessant work and by marrying Julie Löwy, the daughter of a well-to-do brewer, Hermann managed to open a shop in the center of Prague. He evidently had much more self-assurance than sensitivity. He reared his son with rough playfulness (chasing the boy round the table) and exaggerated threats which could terrify an imaginative child ("I'll tear you apart like a fish!"). Kafka recalls an incident when he, as a small child, woke his parents by wailing in the middle of the night, whereupon his father lifted him out of bed and deposited him on the back porch of their house, making Kafka feel, at least in retrospect, as if he were nothing at all, compared to his father. Hermann Kafka dominated both the household and his shop with what his son calls "tyranny," criticizing the children with heavy sarcasm, and speaking brutally to and about his employees. That he treated the latter high-handedly is corroborated by the occasion when they all gave notice and Franz had to visit them individually and persuade them to return. We get a consistent picture of someone whose skills in dealing with people, whether at home or at work, would not rate highly by today's standards. What Kafka does not and cannot convey, of course, is the frustration Hermann Kafka must have felt at people's failure to obey his self-evidently sensible orders, and his sense of estrangement from his own children, especially from Franz and his unconventional youngest daughter, Ottla. Nor does Franz's letter acknowledge the emotional investment Hermann and Julie Kafka must have made in their only surviving son (the other two having died aged fifteen months and six months, respectively), which helps to explain their disappointment with him. They had a standard of success in Franz's first cousin Bruno Kafka, a distinguished professor of law and later a prominent political figure. Instead, Franz grew up with eccentric interests, indifferent professional success, and no apparent ability to marry and found a household.

Franz Kafka's parents, Julie (née Löwy) and Hermann.

Kafka, by his own account, felt overwhelmed by his father. Hermann Kafka's massive body (which would seem huge to a child), noisy self-confidence, and absolute authority made him seem like a giant. "I was oppressed by your sheer corporeality," Kafka writes, recalling how, when they changed at the swimming baths, his father's bulk made him seem "a little skeleton, uncertain, barefoot on the planks, afraid of the water, unable to imitate your strokes." At table Hermann Kafka would devour the food, piping hot, in large mouthfuls, crunching the bones while forbidding the others to do so. (We can see here the origin of the many brutal flesh-eating characters in Kafka's fiction, from the gluttonous Green in *The Man Who Disappeared* to the cannibal in a draft of "A Fasting Artist.") As he grew older, Kafka found his body growing too tall and thin, and he felt uncomfortable in his gangling frame. His lack of physical self-confidence, compared with his father, was only part of a wider insecurity. His father offered a model of adult self-assurance which could never be emulated. Franz started to stutter in his presence, and eventually tried to avoid speaking to him at all. In issuing commands but himself disregarding them, his father seemed to exercise an absolute authority based ultimately on personal charisma. Thanks to this power, Hermann Kafka could denounce everyone, regardless of consistency or logic, and remain unchallengeable. "For me you acquired the mysterious quality possessed by all tyrants whose rights are founded on their person and not on their ideas. At least that was how it seemed to me." His father seemed to occupy the whole of life, like a figure sprawled across the map of the world, leaving no room for Franz. Unable to imitate his father, Kafka was left blaming himself for his inability, according to his own summary: "Because of you, I lost my self-confidence and acquired a boundless feeling of guilt in exchange."

The area where Hermann Kafka dominated most securely was marriage. He was married; Franz was not but was expected to marry. The adult Kafka interprets this situation as a double bind.

If I want to attain independence in the particular unhappy relationship I have with you, I need to do something that has the least possible connection with you; marrying is the greatest thing and gives the most creditable independence, but at the same time it is most closely connected with you.

What Kafka formulates here is the classic Oedipal relationship as described by Freud. To become adult, a male has to become like his father, a sexually mature being; but he must also resist his father by displacing him from the position of sole, or supreme, sexually mature male in the household. To emulate his father, he must oppose his father. Franz had the added difficulty that as a boy he was, by his own account, so uninterested in sex as to be prudishly offended by any mention of it, whereas Hermann Kafka called a spade a spade: a hint by his father that he ought to visit a brothel seemed to the teenage Franz "the dirtiest thing there was." So, according to Kafka, his own wish to find a partner was blocked by the negative forces—weakness, insecurity, guilt, low self-esteem—implanted in him by his father.

How else could Kafka, according to himself, have escaped from his father's influence? One possibility was a career, and Kafka does acknowledge that his parents allowed him to study whatever he wanted. (That was not trivial. University study meant continuing to live at home, without earning, for a minimum of four years, followed by a considerable period before he would earn enough to help his parents or set up house himself.) But the freedom implied in this permission, according to Kafka, was nullified in advance. For his overwhelming sense of guilt prevented him from enjoying his school studies, so convinced was he that he would fail the exam at the end of each year. And though he always passed, he could be interested in his studies only (as he puts it) to the extent that a bank official who has defrauded his employers can be interested in day-to-day transactions while he waits to be found out. So, since every subject was unattractive, he might as well study one—law—which was completely repellent. "In the months before the exams," Kafka recalls bitterly, "I suffered great nervous tension and lived on an intellectual diet of sawdust, which, moreover, had been previously chewed by a thousand mouths." Although Kafka presents his choice with such perverse and masochistic reasoning, for anyone without definite plans or interests the study of law was the obvious university course to choose, since it admitted one to a wide range of careers in the courts, industry, commerce, finance, and the public services.

An obvious way to escape from Hermann's world seemed to be through literature. And writing, Kafka admits, did bring some relief. But it did not bring freedom, because what had he to write about? "All my writing was about you; I only lamented there the things I couldn't lament on your breast." This is of course an exaggeration. Overwhelming fathers do appear in *The Judgment* and *The Transformation*. One condemns his son to death by drowning; the other pelts his son (now in insect form) with apples and causes him a fatal wound. Even so, creating such figures, half-terrifying and half-ridiculous, is clearly Kafka's way of gaining distance from and control of his own situation. In the letter, however, Kafka, without citing specific passages, chooses to present all his writing as another form of dependence. The flight from life into literature must fail because literature has to be about life.

How does the "Letter to His Father" rate as self-analysis? It presents the writer, in a highly dramatic but broadly plausible way, as someone whose self-esteem has been severely damaged by an insensitive upbringing and by a sense of disappointing his parents' expectations. That he feels his failure so strongly, of course, shows just how much Kafka has internalized his parents' expectations. He too feels that he ought to marry and start a family, but he wants to because his parents want him to. Kafka is astute in identifying the double bind in which his relationship with his father has placed him. He charges his father with expecting him to marry, yet shaping his character in such a way that he could not marry. But he may not quite see how far his whole letter expresses and confirms this double bind. The letter may have been written to free himself from his father's influence, but Kafka portrays himself as so utterly his father's creation that escape from his father is unthinkable.

We may be surprised by the tiny role that Kafka's mother plays in this letter. She appears only as an assistant to the father, too close to him ever to afford the children any protection from his authority, but nevertheless as an unhappy mediator, oppressed by her husband and by the children. "We hammered at her ruthlessly, you from your side, we from ours." In the two stories that bear the clearest relation to Kafka's own domestic life, the mother in *The Judgment* is dead, and her counterpart in *The Transformation*, though devoted to her "unfortunate son," is ineffectual and can be relied upon only to faint in a crisis. It is, however, likely, in the view of psychoanalysts, that Kafka's emotional vulnerability resulted not only from his father's dominance but also from his mother's early withdrawal of affection from him. His diaries present Julie Kafka as "whimpering" about her son's oddities, arousing his irritation, and entirely failing to understand him: he complains that she took him for an ordinary young man who would presently put aside his whims and marry and found a family like everyone else. Their estrangement, and their underlying affection, emerge from a touching moment recorded in a postscript to a letter to Felice:

> I was just going to get undressed when my mother came in because of something trivial and, as she was leaving, offered me a good-night kiss, which hasn't happened for many years. "That's right," I said. "I never dared," said my mother, "I thought you didn't like it. But if you like it, so do I."

The "Letter" is not to be dismissed. It contains a great deal of actual experience and perceptive self-analysis. But in large measure it is a story—a story such as Kafka told himself about his own life. That is no objection: perhaps the best that even psychoanalysis can provide is a satisfying story of how we became who we are. Still, it does bring the "Letter" closer to Kafka's fictional narratives about guilt, from *The Man Who Disappeared* onward. Indeed, we can see Kafka's imagination inventing the comparison with the fraudulent banker, which sounds like the germ of another novel like *The Trial*.

Getting Married

Two matters that bulk hugely in Kafka's life are touched on in the "Letter" but deserve further exploration. One is his fruitless wish to marry; the other is the importance his writing had for him.

Kafka talked and behaved as if getting married were the central project of his life.

> To marry, to found a family, to accept all the children that arrive, support them in this uncertain world and even guide

them a little, is in my belief the utmost that anybody can possibly achieve.

Yet this sentence from the "Letter to His Father" is curiously impersonal. It describes not Kafka's own, personally chosen ambition, but "anybody's." When he tried to achieve it, he not only found himself in the familial double bind that he himself recognized; he also replicated this double bind by his choice of partner. Felice Bauer, four years his junior, was an intelligent, well-read, extremely able professional woman. Kafka admired her, but sexual attraction, or even pleasure in her company, seem hardly to have existed. After spending time with her in January 1915, Kafka wrote in his diary: "Except in letters, I never felt with F. the sweetness of a relationship with a beloved woman, as in Zuckmantel and Riva, only boundless admiration." The relationships he had had when on holiday in the resorts of Zuckmantel in 1905 and Riva in 1913 were casual, untroubled affairs. The prospect of marriage to the supremely competent Felice, however, confirmed Kafka's sense of inadequacy. It also meant replicating the stifling family life in which he had grown up. Felice took him shopping for furniture, which made him think of tombstones, and insisted that their flat must have a "personal touch," a phrase Kafka hated. At the official engagement, he felt "bound like a criminal." His more than five hundred letters and postcards to her betray an immense emotional neediness, a desire to know about her life which suggests a wish for control, and a strange lack of intimacy. He seems not to have known about the problems in the Bauer family with which Felice had to cope: her parents had been estranged for several years during which her father lived with his mistress; her brother was

Kafka and Felice Bauer, to whom he was engaged twice, in 1914 and 1917. Both engagements were broken.

a swindler who eventually fled to America; and only Felice knew that her unmarried elder sister was pregnant. Although Felice's letters have not survived, it is safe to assume that she found Kafka, though attractive and interesting, also exasperating; she broke off the engagement on July 12, 1914, though they stayed in touch and got engaged again in July 1917.

Of Kafka's other relationships, that with Milena shows a similar pattern of casting himself as inadequate, though Milena was intellectually far more in sympathy with him, and his letters to her are far more confiding than those to Felice. Their keynote is insecurity, fear, and an extraordinary self-denigration. He compares himself to a man dying on a filthy bed who receives a visit from the Angel of Death, "the most beatific of all angels." This time, though, we also have the woman's view of the relationship. Both during and after the relationship, she wrote about Kafka to Max Brod, complaining of his impracticality in small things like going to a post office counter, and of his naive admiration for other people just because they were competent (including Felice and even Milena's husband, the expert seducer Ernst Polak), but she also credited Kafka with a mystical apprehension of the world as infinitely strange, and paid tribute to his exceptional character:

He also thinks he is the one who is guilty and weak, and yet there is nobody else in the world with his immense strength: this absolute, unchallengeable need for perfection, for purity and for truth.

A different pattern in Kafka's emotional life is his attraction to younger women who did not invite the helpless idealization that Felice and Milena did. Not much is known about Julie Wohryzek, whom he met on holiday in 1919. It was his father's disapproval of their brief engagement that provoked Kafka's "Letter." Once he was involved with Milena, Kafka ended things with Julie, to her distress: "Are you really sending me away?" she said. Much more promising was Kafka's relationship with Dora Diamant, whom we now know to be as remarkable a person as Felice and Milena. Kafka met her on holiday in August 1923. Dora was then twenty-five, fifteen years younger than Kafka, and living independently in Berlin. She shared his increasing interest in Zionism and Jewish culture, and they planned to emigrate to Palestine, where they might open a restaurant, with Dora as cook and Kafka as waiter. It never happened, but she did help Kafka to break away from his family and from Prague, and to spend perhaps the happiest period of his life in Berlin before his tuberculosis caught up with him. Afterward Dora became a

Married Czech journalist Milena Jesenská (1896–1944), with whom Kafka had a short affair, translated some of Kafka's work into Czech.

noted actress and an active Communist (as did Milena), who emigrated first to the Soviet Union and then to Britain, dying in London in 1952.

Kafka's difficulties with relationships, documented in lengthy, often obsessive letters and diary entries, naturally bulk large in posterity's image of him. Some facile explanations have been suggested, including the claim that he was really homosexual. While this presupposes a rather crude notion of gender identity, there is no doubt that Kafka's imagination does have a homoerotic dimension. In life, he enjoyed literary and sporting meetings with all-male groups including his friends Max Brod and Franz Werfel (the portly boy wonder of Prague German literature). He was aware of the widespread celebration of male physical culture which found expression in the Wandervogel movement, which sent young people hiking across Germany, and he read with enthusiasm the book on male bonding by the Wandervogel leader Hans Blüher. On November 20, 1917, he writes merrily to Brod: "If I add that recently I kissed Werfel in a dream, I shall fall right into Blüher's book." In this circle, affection between men could be expressed, verbally at least, without embarrassment: thus in several letters Kafka thanks Brod for presents by saying "I kiss you." Homoerotic friendship clearly binds Karl Rossmann and the Stoker in the first chapter of *The Man Who Disappeared* (which Kafka had no scruples about publishing separately as *The Stoker*); the fragment "On the Kalda Railway" places its protagonist in the center of Russia in an isolation broken only by occasional visits from the Inspector which include homosexual embraces; and the culminating scene of *The Castle* includes K.'s dream in which a Castle secretary appears naked as a Greek god ("Greek" being a standard code for male homosexuality). Conversely, Kafka's fiction portrays heterosexual intercourse as frightening and nasty. In *The Man Who Disappeared*, the thuggish Klara makes sexual advances to Karl and then throws him down by "ju-jitsu." The animal-like Leni in *The Trial*, with her webbed fingers, seduces Josef K. by dragging him down to the floor and proclaiming: "Now you belong to me." Worst of all, in *The Castle* K. and Frieda make love among the puddles on the barroom floor, and yet the latter encounter is described in lyrical language, suggesting that sex, though dirty, can also express love and self-loss. Kafka told Milena that his sexual drive made him feel like the Wandering Jew, "senselessly drawn, senselessly wandering through a senselessly dirty world," but also that sex had "something of the air that was breathed in Paradise before the Fall." Passages like these show how pointless it is to put a label on Kafka's sexual imagination. Instead, one should read and re-read his writings on the subject, to appreciate the emotional honesty with which he holds together a range of feelings that are singularly hard to articulate.

"I Consist of Literature"

When Kafka contemplated marriage, the main obstacle was his devotion to writing. It is hardly possible to exaggerate how important writing was for him. He barely does so when he tells Felice (after she had shown his handwriting to a graphologist who had detected "literary interests"): "I do not have literary interests, I consist of literature, I am nothing else and cannot be anything else." He feared that marriage would destroy the solitude he needed for writing. When she suggested that she could sit beside him while he wrote, he replied by fantasizing a life at a writing desk in the innermost room of an extensive cellar, interrupted only by walks to fetch his meals from outside the cellar door. Even when solitude was available, writing was difficult and frustrating. Kafka's diaries are full of stories that peter out after a page or less, and of lamentations and self-reproaches at his inability to write. Only occasionally did he manage to write successfully and without conscious effort. The greatest such occasion was the night of September 22–23, 1912, when from 10 p.m. to 6 a.m. he sat at his desk writing *The Judgment* in a single sitting. "That is the *only* way to write," he told his diary the next day, "only with such coherence, with such complete opening of body and soul." This literary breakthrough occurred a month after he first met Felice, and he told Brod that while finishing the story he thought of a powerful ejaculation; the story's last word is "*Verkehr*," which in the context means "road traffic" but can also mean "(sexual) intercourse." Was his sexuality, aroused by Felice, diverted into his writing?

Not only was successful writing an intensely pleasurable experience, but writing enabled Kafka to gain distance from the painful events in his life. Often, an unpleasant experience spurred his creativity. Thus he wrote *The Trial* and *In the Penal Colony* in the months following the dissolution of his engagement, in a scene which he described in his diary as a "tribunal" (anticipating the metaphor of justice which structures both stories), and began *The Castle* when his relationship with Milena was reaching its end. By writing, he could escape futile self-analysis through assuming a higher perspective. The consolation of writing, he noted in 1922, was that it enabled him to leap out of the "line of killers," in which every action was immediately nullified by self-observation, and to create "a higher kind of observation, a higher, not a sharper one, and the higher it is, the more inaccessible from the 'line,' the more it follows its own laws of motion, the more incalculable, joyous and ascending is its path." In addition, he felt that his writing was more than self-therapy. It expressed its epoch. Admitting to his publisher in 1916 that *In the Penal Colony* was a "painful" story, he explained "that our epoch, and my time in particular, are very painful." Latterly he interpreted his writing as an enigmatic mission. "I can still have temporary satisfaction from works like *A Country Doctor*," he noted in 1917, "assuming I achieve anything more of the sort (very unlikely); but happiness only if I can raise the world into the pure, the true, the unchangeable." Whatever this means, it is clear that he attached more than personal importance to his writing.

In his devotion to writing, Kafka acknowledged a number of models and heroes. His literary blood-relatives, he said, were Flaubert, Dostoevsky, Kleist, and Grillparzer. He read them avidly, including their personal writings, and often identified with aspects of their lives. In the case of Grillparzer, Kafka was not interested in the plays that made him Austria's greatest dramatist, but in his story "The Poor Minstrel" (1847) about a sincere but misguided devotion to art, and in his long relationship with a woman whom he could never bring himself to marry. Dostoevsky's exile in Siberia contributed to the imagery of penal servitude and bound criminals that occurred to Kafka when he became engaged. As for Flaubert, two quotations seemed particularly applicable to Kafka himself. One was Flaubert's statement in a letter

Austrian dramatist Franz Grillparzer (1791–1872), shown here in a statue in the Volksgarten in Vienna, wrote the short story "Der arme Spielmann" ("The Poor Minstrel") in 1847.

to George Sand on September 9, 1868, when he was struggling to finish *L'education sentimentale*, Kafka's favorite among his works, "My novel is the rock to which I cling, and I know nothing of what is happening in the world," which matched Kafka's own needy devotion to writing. The other is a remark recorded by Flaubert's niece Caroline Commanville (who visited Prague in 1909 and was interviewed by Brod). After Caroline had taken him to visit a married friend with a large family, Flaubert said ruefully: "*Ils sont dans le vrai*"—"They are in the truth." This perfectly conveyed Kafka's feeling of the immeasurable loss, as well as the gain, involved in his devotion to literature.

Kafka considered French novelist Gustave Flaubert (1821–80), shown here in an undated photograph, a literary blood-relative.

More generally, Kafka was an avid reader, and kept up with contemporary literature by subscribing to the *Neue Rundschau* (*New Review*), the leading literary periodical of its day. The review's taste was mildly conservative, like Kafka's. He did not care for the stridency of the young Expressionist writers. He admired precision, economy, and understatement, especially in short prose sketches such as those by Peter Altenberg and Robert Walser, and in short fiction like that of Chekhov and the early Thomas Mann. It may be surprising that he also enjoyed Dickens, but he was impressed by sheer overflowing energy, especially since he felt its lack. And his favorite books included boys' adventure stories, available in the series called Schaffstein's Little Green

Books, including narratives by a German sugar planter and by a soldier who witnessed Napoleon's campaigns in Russia. He was also a keen cinema-goer who enjoyed a Western (*Slaves of Gold*), a thriller about prostitution (*The White Slave*), and a tear-jerker (*Little Lolotte*). A reference in a letter of January 1924 to Chaplin's *The Kid*, then showing in Berlin, leaves it tantalizingly uncertain whether Kafka knew at first hand the master of straight-faced slapstick whose work has so often been compared to his.

It is often thought that, spending almost all his life in Prague, Kafka was isolated from the European literary scene, whether geographically or linguistically. As a Jew whose native language was German, in a city and province where the majority language was Czech, he is sometimes said to have inhabited a threefold ghetto. That is not accurate.

Chaplin's *The Kid*, in which Chaplin's Little Tramp finds and cares for an abandoned child (Jackie Coogan), debuted in the United States in 1921. Kafka may have seen it in Berlin three years later.

The German-speaking, largely middle-class minority in Prague had their own schools, theaters, and newspapers, and in 1882 the ancient Charles University had been divided into a German-speaking and a Czech-speaking institution, but the German speakers, far from living in a single ghettolike area, were interspersed with Czech speakers, and one could not even have gone shopping without a working knowledge of Czech. Their numbers were dwindling: between 1880 and 1910 the population of Prague rose from 260,000 to 442,000, but the number of German speakers (that is, of people who identified themselves thus on census forms) sank from 38,600 (14.6 percent) to 32,300 (7.3 percent). Kafka spoke, read, and wrote Czech fluently, though not perfectly, and sometimes attended the Czech National Theater. His German had some peculiarities of the southern German language zone (such as *mittagmahlen* and *nachtmahlen* for having lunch and dinner), and some features peculiar to Prague (like *paar* for *ein Paar*, "a few"), but he neither spoke nor wrote "Prague German," a dialect imagined a century ago by German nationalists who thought that only country-dwellers, being close to the soil, could speak an authentic language and that city-dwellers must speak an etiolated and impoverished tongue. The German of his published texts is precise, correct, and modeled on classic German prose.

Kafka belonged to an important generation of German-language writers from Prague, including his friends Brod and Werfel, and the somewhat older Rainer Maria Rilke. Though they were citizens of the Austro-Hungarian Empire, the cultural centers that interested them were not Vienna, but Berlin and the publishing capital Leipzig. Rilke, considering Austria a backwater, moved to Berlin in 1897; Werfel moved to Leipzig in 1912. Brod's first novel, *Schloss Nornepygge* (1908),

The city gate and tower on Charles Bridge in Prague.

appeared in Leipzig and gained him a high reputation (now hard to understand) among the Berlin avant-garde. Kafka's first book, *Meditation* (1912), was published in Leipzig by Ernst Rowohlt, whose publishing house was then taken over by the young and enterprising Kurt Wolff, who specialized in promoting avant-garde writers, especially those from Prague. During his lifetime Kafka published seven small books: *Meditation, The Stoker, The Judgment, The Transformation, In the Penal Colony, A Country Doctor: Little Tales,* and *A Fasting Artist: Four Stories.* They brought him modest fame. Robert Musil, later well-known for

The Man Without Qualities (1930–43), wrote an appreciative review of *Meditation* and *The Stoker* in the *New Review*, of which he had just become editor, and invited Kafka to contribute, an invitation that Kafka had to decline because he had nothing suitable to hand. In 1915 the prestigious Fontane Prize for prose fiction was awarded to Carl Sternheim (now best remembered for his hilarious comedy *The Knickers*, 1911), who, being already a millionaire, was easily persuaded to pass the prize on to Kafka, whose work he admired. Authors often publicize their work by public readings: Kafka seems to have read from his own work only twice, presenting *The Judgment* on December 4, 1912, to a literary society in Prague, and on November 10, 1916, reading *In the Penal Colony* in the Goltz Art Gallery in Munich; the latter occasion was attended by Rilke, who complimented Kafka afterward. So he was far from obscure during his lifetime, and the posthumous publication of his novels in the 1920s did not radically change his reputation. Although his books are popularly supposed to have been burned by the Nazis in 1933, I can find no evidence that they paid any attention to him.

Kafka's international reputation began when Willa and Edwin Muir translated his works into English, beginning with *The Castle* in 1930. It took off more slowly in France: Alexandre Vialatte's translation of *The Trial*, *Le Procès*, appeared in 1933, his *Le Château* in 1938. The surge in his reputation as quintessential expositor of the spiritual plight of modern man is especially an Anglo-American phenomenon. It was famously formulated by W. H. Auden in 1941:

> Had one to name the artist who comes nearest to bearing the same kind of relation to our age that Dante, Shakespeare and Goethe bore to theirs, Kafka is the first one would think of.

Such a view is easy to criticize. It was encouraged by Max Brod's hagiographic memoir, first published in 1937 and translated into English in 1947, which portrayed Kafka as having a constructive spiritual message for distressed moderns, and it was exploited by Gustav Janouch in his *Conversations with Kafka*, first published in 1951, which are so shameless in making Kafka pontificate on modern ills that the few possibly authentic materials are submerged; Janouch's book, though often credulously cited as evidence of what Kafka really thought, is best regarded as spurious.

Nevertheless, Kafka's slender oeuvre has proved to be a modern classic. It can be read and re-read, always disclosing something new, and it offers material for every school of criticism, from existentialism and structuralism down to postcolonialism. The apparent versatility of his work confirms its greatness, for a classic work is precisely one that can be viewed afresh from every new angle. How Kafka's literary work shapes and articulates matters of pressing concern to his readers will be the subject of the following chapters. But it is not my aim to decode Kafka or say baldly what Kafka's work is "about." There is no way into Kafka except by reading Kafka and puzzling over Kafka. The next chapter will therefore consider, not so much what Kafka's texts mean, but rather how they ask to be read.

TWO

Reading Kafka

•

Kafka as Conservative Modernist

Reading Kafka is a puzzling experience. Impossible events occur with an air of inevitability, and no explanation is forthcoming. Gregor Samsa is turned into an insect, without knowing how or why. Josef K. never learns the reason for his arrest. The other K. never reaches the Castle and does not understand why he cannot meet the official who (perhaps) summoned him there as a land surveyor.

Not only are the characters bewildered: so is the reader. As in the cinema, events are shown only from the viewpoint of the main character. With very rare exceptions, we see only what he sees. As early as 1934 Theodor Adorno wrote that Kafka's novels read like texts accompanying silent films. The reader's knowledge is similarly limited. We learn no more

Anthony Perkins in *The Trial* (1962), a film by Orson Welles based on Kafka's novel.

than the central character knows about his situation, and therefore share his bewilderment. When Josef K. has his bedroom invaded by a strange man apparently in uniform, or when he discovers that the Court offices are situated in attics, the reader is as surprised as he is. Nor (with very rare exceptions) is the reader given any additional information about the characters or their experiences. When we are told that Josef K. was "inclined to take everything as easily as possible," we see, if we look closely, that this is actually part of Josef K.'s thoughts, not information given by the narrator, and therefore it is to be regarded with the same distrust as everything else that the defendant Josef K. says about himself.

Why does Kafka disorient the reader in this way? In part, he is taking to an extreme a widespread tendency of modern literature. Many years ago Roland Barthes distinguished modern from earlier literature by asserting that the former produces writerly texts (*textes scriptibles*), the latter readerly texts (*textes lisibles*). By a "readerly text" Barthes meant one for which an authoritative interpretation already exists and has simply to be accepted by the reader, whereas a "writerly text" has no definite interpretation and invites the reader to participate actively in making sense of the text. Barthes in turn adapted this distinction from Brecht, who claimed that all theater before his own was "culinary," requiring the spectator simply to sit back and consume the drama in a passive emotional trance, whereas Brecht's own theater demanded active involvement from a spectator who should be critical or even outraged. Of course, both Brecht and Barthes were indulging in polemical oversimplifications. Nineteenth-century realism, the target of Barthes's enmity, demands a much more alert and attentive reading than he was willing to admit. But one can see the point of his distinction if one thinks of Dickens or Trollope, in whose writing good and bad characters are for the most part easy to identify. In such a modernist text as Conrad's *Lord Jim*, however, character and motivation are ambiguous. The question why Jim jumped ship, abandoning the passengers to likely death, cannot be explained by any simple moral or psychological scheme, and to explore it Conrad needs his narrator, Marlow, who mediates between the enigmatic Jim and the puzzled reader.

Kafka's work can be compared to that of British novelist Joseph Conrad (1857–1924), shown here in a photograph taken in 1916, in its focus on uncertainty, ambiguity, and perplexity.

Kafka may be compared to Conrad in that both are conservative modernists, indebted to nineteenth-century models, providing superficially readable narratives, but perplexing the attentive reader with psychological and epistemological enigmas. Kafka, like Conrad, focuses on uncertainty, ambiguity, perplexity. Unlike Conrad, however, he has no Marlow figure, no narrator to conduct inquiries on behalf of the reader. If one is puzzled by Kafka, it is not because one has somehow missed the point: Kafka's texts are puzzling. And they are so because uncertainty and perplexity are essential features of the reality Kafka is writing about. His first book, the collection of short prose sketches entitled *Meditation*, includes "The Passenger," the first paragraph of which runs:

> I am standing on the platform of the tram and am entirely uncertain with regard to my place in this world, in this town, in my family. Not even approximately could I state what claims I might justifiably advance in any direction. I am quite unable to defend the fact that I am standing on this platform, holding on to this strap, letting myself be carried along by this tram, and that people are getting out of the tram's way or walking along quietly or pausing in front of the shop windows.—Not that anyone asks me to, but that is immaterial. [translation modified]

The juddering platform of the moving tram provides a metaphor for the lack of any fixed reference point either in the immediate setting of the family or the outermost horizon represented by "the world." And as the German original specifies that it is an electric tram (in contrast to the earlier horse-drawn trams), this uncertainty appears to be something new, characteristic of modernity. Beside his lack of bearings and his deficient sense of belonging, the speaker feels a strange need for justification, expressed in oddly official, legal language: "in regard to," "approximately," "advance claims," "defend." He cannot "defend" the most casual action, like straphanging in the tram. Nor can he "defend" the casual behavior of the people in the streets. Why should such things need defending? We are not told, but it is typical of Kafka that by using a word that seems inappropriate to its context he should evoke a different way of looking at the familiar world. Perhaps the world is not just an assemblage of people and objects, but also an entity requiring some—moral? legal? religious?—justification for its existence, and that justification has now vanished, or become impossible to find. In this unassuming paragraph we can find the seeds of *The Trial*, in which an average professional man is called to account before a mysterious Court, and of *The Castle*, in which another professional man tries vainly to obtain assurance about his place in society.

The sketches in *Meditation* evoke a mood rather than tell a story. Kafka's task was to give this uncertainty a narrative equivalent, and he managed it in the text that for him marked a literary breakthrough, *The Judgment*, written in September 1912. At first, the story appears to be a realist text, set in a world that obeys familiar rules of time, space, causality, and coherence. A young man, already a successful businessman, is writing to a friend in Russia about his engagement. Nothing extraordinary there, though we might wonder about the emotional block that has prevented Georg from breaking the news to his friend until now. Having finished the letter, Georg goes to the back of the flat to show the letter to his old and infirm father. Although his father's responses seem slightly off the point, there is nothing really surprising until he asks Georg the question: "Have you really got this friend in St Petersburg?" Instead of giving a straight answer, Georg seems to interpret this question as a reproach for neglecting his father by planning to get married. With every appearance of loving care, he picks up his father, carries him to bed, and tucks him up. Then comes the change: Georg's father, previously decrepit, leaps upright on the bed, towers over Georg, and accuses him of all manner of selfish and ruthless behavior toward his parents and his friend. Finally he sentences the increasingly helpless Georg to death by drowning, and Georg rushes out of the flat to the nearby river and jumps off a bridge. By now realism has been left behind. The father's recovery of strength is realistically impossible; the behavior he ascribes to Georg sounds like a paranoid fantasy; the very existence of the friend in Russia is in doubt; and the death sentence, and its execution, defy belief. Yet the events, as they unfold rapidly, carry absolute conviction. When old resentments suddenly surface, any material, irrespective of its factual truth, will serve to express their emotional passion. We are now in the territory of Expressionism, the German variant of modernism, which sought not to depict familiar reality but to disrupt it in order to portray forces underlying it through powerful images. The image of the father in his nightshirt, at once accuser and judge, too terrifying to be ridiculous, is as memorable as anything the Expressionists invented. And the verdict he pronounces on his son explicitly distinguishes between surface reality and a deeper truth: "You were an innocent child, it's true, but it's even more true that you've been a devilish human being!"

To explain how Kafka puzzles the reader in *The Judgment*, we could think of a fictional contract. Normally a writer enters into an implicit contract with the reader about the kind of text that will be supplied. The title and the opening sentences usually indicate whether we are getting (for example) an autobiographical tale, a romance, a mystery, or an adventure story, and what laws will govern its fictional reality: whether it will stick to our normal standards of plausibility, or whether it will include ghosts, fairies, or aliens. The expectations thus established are what we call the genre and mode of a literary work. Kafka breaks his fictional contract. He first makes us think that *The Judgment* is a realist text, then turns it into an Expressionist nightmare. And this breach of faith with the reader is not merely wanton. It corresponds to a real uncertainty about what sort of world we are living in. Can the world be adequately represented by the realism of the opening, with the businessman's reflections on his marriage plans and his financial success ("the turnover had increased fivefold")? Are there not aspects of reality that cannot be calculated in this way, and cannot be represented by this surface realism—passion, envy, hatred? The reality of passions needs Expressionist images of power and conflict. And beyond that, there may be another aspect of reality, signaled by the father's god-like role as judge and by such textual hints as the maidservant's cry "Jesus!" when Georg rushes downstairs on his way to execute himself. But the religious element in the story is not expressed in any coherent way. A mode of writing that coherently relates earthly events to the timeless realities of religion is called allegory. But Kafka does not write allegory. It would be impossible, for example, to read *The Judgment* as an allegory in which Georg stands for Jesus. Yet even if literature no longer has any coherent way of representing such realities, that does not mean that they no longer exist or no longer have any claim on our attention. They therefore appear in Kafka's writing as a series of hints and allusions which fracture the surface of the text and remind us yet again that any literary mode is only a provisional and inadequate way of representing reality.

In *The Judgment*, then, Kafka defies the expectations of readers that a text will have a stable relation to reality—that it will stay in the same literary mode throughout. Instead, Kafka begins in the realist mode and moves to the Expressionist mode, with hints of a further reality that neither can accommodate. The resulting bafflement corresponds to a perplexity about the kind of world we do in fact live in. Can the world be calculated and predicted, as is assumed by the young capitalist Georg (and by the realist novel, which developed together with capitalism)? Is the world ruled by powerful, unpredictable emotions, based in the biological realities of family life? Is our world connected to another, timeless reality which can be represented by the language and symbols of religion? Anyone might be puzzled by these questions, especially as the answer to all three may be yes. Kafka has not supplied an answer; he has found a fictional means of keeping all three questions open.

Realism and/or Expressionism

Two months after completing *The Judgment*, Kafka set to work on *The Transformation*. While the earlier story began in the realist mode and moved into the Expressionist mode, *The Transformation* deploys both simultaneously.

> When Gregor Samsa awoke one morning from troubled dreams he found himself transformed in his bed into a monstrous insect. He was lying on his hard shell-like back and by lifting his head a little he could see his curved brown belly, divided by stiff arching ribs, on top of which the bed-quilt was precariously poised and seemed about to slide off completely. His numerous legs, which

were pathetically thin compared to the rest of his body, danced helplessly before his eyes.

The huge insect is as striking an image as those devised by Expressionist painters, poets, and playwrights. Franz Marc's blue horses, the savage gods in Georg Heym's poems "War" and "The God of the City," or the dictatorial Engineer in Georg Kaiser's play *Gas* all demand that we look through the familiar surface of reality to discern the forces churning beneath it. The insect image may similarly suggest that, just as Georg Bendemann was truly "a devilish human being," Gregor is truly an insect— disgusting to himself and others, despised, in constant danger of being crushed by his oppressive family and employers. But while Expressionist writers convey their visions through strident verbal violence, Kafka's language is remarkably sober and descriptive. Even the word *monstrous* primarily denotes the insect's size. Its back, belly, and legs are described in such meticulous, almost scientific detail that some readers—notably Vladimir Nabokov, who was an entomologist as well as a novelist and critic—have been moved to draw the insect and to speculate about its species. So we have an Expressionist image conveyed in realistic detail. Similarly, the reactions of Gregor's family to the impossible but undeniable transformation of their son and brother are remarkably matter-of-fact. They confine him to his room, swear the servants to secrecy, try to find out what he will now eat, and use his room to store junk. And finally, with an all-too-human illogic, they conclude that the insect is not, or no longer, Gregor and collude in its/his death.

However, Kafka's compromise between realism and Expressionism is tilted a little further away from realism. In calling the transformed Gregor an "insect," the translator and I have been cheating. The word

German Expressionist painter Franz Marc created his *Tower of Blue Horses*, an oil on canvas, in 1913.

Kafka uses is *Ungeziefer*, a much vaguer term meaning "vermin" or a "pest," connoting harmfulness and nastiness rather than identifying any actual creature. The description, if we read it attentively, does not quite make sense. If his belly is arched, then, when he crawls, how do his little legs reach the ground? Moreover, Kafka insisted to his publisher that the "insect" (as he did call it in a letter) could not and must not be depicted. The cover illustration for *The Transformation* instead shows a young man staggering away from the door that leads into a dark room, an image that does not actually match any event in the text. Unlike Conrad, who famously wrote (in the Preface to *The Nigger of the "Narcissus,"* 1897) "My task [. . .] is, before all, to make you see," Kafka does not want to make us see but to bewilder us in our attempts at fictional visualization.

Moreover, the description of Gregor's invertebrate body is less neutral than the term "realism" might imply. His little legs look "helpless" and "pathetic." The bed quilt is comically poised atop his belly, about to slide off—a cartoon-like detail, recalling how the transformed father in *The Judgment* "flung back the blanket with such force that for an instant it unfurled flat in the air." So the description is charged with emotions of

First-edition title page of Kafka's *Die Verwandlung* (*The Transformation*) (1915).

a sort difficult to reconcile. Pathos and comedy together point toward a subdued black humor. It is not so much *what* you see, but *how* you see it, that concerns Kafka. And that too is a complex matter. Gregor registers his transformation without being able to assimilate such a revolution in his existence. His next action is to look out of the window, notice the rain, and feel quite melancholy, as if the weather were his worst problem. The following pages recount in minute detail how Gregor, summoned to work, promises (in an unintelligible animal-like voice) to get up, and struggles out of bed and to the door, manipulating his unfamiliar body without consciously realizing what he is doing. The focus of the story is not so much the transformation as Gregor's delayed response to his transformation.

This focus confirms Kafka's distance from realism. Realism presupposes an agreement on what reality is. Even though, as George Eliot says in *Middlemarch*, it is always seen from "an equivalent centre of self, whence the lights and shadows must always fall with a certain difference," a consensus exists on the nature of the world that is seen. In Kafka, that consensus has vanished, and seeing becomes problematic. There is no longer a stable reality out there, on which the realist text can offer a window. There are only versions of reality, which may be profoundly inadequate or mistaken, and the narrative focuses on the protagonist's consciousness and his or her attempts to make sense of the world.

Kafka shows his distance from mimetic realism by his treatment of pictures and photographs. In *The Trial*, Josef K. is shown a portrait of a judge, a powerful, bushy-browed figure half rising from his throne as though in denunciation, but then learns that the portrait merely follows convention, the actual judge being a tiny man who sits on a kitchen chair covered with a horse blanket. K. in *The Castle* sees a photograph showing a Castle messenger: at first the young man appears to be lying immobile on a couch; closer inspection reveals that he is leaping over a high horizontal bar in his haste to deliver his message. Even the camera provides no reliable account of the world. Its pictures need to be interpreted as much as any other message.

How much is at stake in this epistemological uncertainty can be seen from the humorous tale "The New Advocate," written in January 1917 and published in the modestly titled collection *A Country Doctor: Little Tales* (1919).

· · · · ·

THE NEW ADVOCATE

We have a new advocate, Dr Bucephalus. In his outward appearance there is little to recall the time when he was still the war-horse of Alexander of Macedon. Anyone who is familiar with the circumstances will notice a thing or two, of course. But the other day, on the forecourt steps, I even saw a quite simple usher lost in admiration as he watched the advocate, with the expert eye of the regular racegoer, climbing up with a high-stepping tread that made each of his steps ring out on the marble.

On the whole the admission of Bucephalus meets with the approval of the Bar. With remarkable insight people tell themselves that Bucephalus is, given the present order of society, in a difficult position, and that he deserves for that reason, as well as on account of his historical importance, at least a sympathetic reception. Today—it cannot be denied—there is no Alexander the Great. There are indeed plenty of those who know how to murder; even the skill required to spear a friend across the banqueting table is not lacking; and many find

Macedonia too constricting, so that they curse Philip the father—but no one, no one can lead the way to India. Even in those days the gates of India were beyond reach, but the royal sword pointed to where they stood. Today the gates have been carried off to some quite other, remoter and loftier places; no one shows the direction; many hold swords in their hands, but only to brandish them, and the eye that tries to follow them grows confused.

So perhaps it really is best to do what Bucephalus has done, and immerse oneself in the books of the law. Free, his flanks unconstrained by the grip of his rider, in the still light of the lamp, far from the din of the Battle of Issus, he reads and turns the pages of our ancient books.

· · · · ·

This is another tale of transformation, only Bucephalus has moved in the opposite direction from Gregor. While Gregor has regressed from human to insect form, Bucephalus has advanced from being a warhorse to being a human lawyer. Or has he? There is "little to recall" his career as a charger; only "a thing or two" distinguishes Bucephalus from a human; yet he raises his legs high like a horse, his steps "ring" as though his hooves are still shod, and a regular racegoer is able to admire his equine qualities. As he sits studying his legal tomes, he feels his "flanks" free from "the grip of his rider." To inquire further—to ask, for example, how he turns the pages with his hooves—would spoil the joke.

The serious questions underlying the joke become apparent as the story's tone moves from fussy officialese to elegiac regret. First, the impossibility of visualizing Bucephalus corresponds to the impossibility, since Darwin, of distinguishing finally between human beings and animals, and hence of defining what it is to be human. Gregor may have slid down the evolutionary ladder; Bucephalus may have mounted up it: for both it is a continuum, with no line marking off humanity as distinct. Kafka grew up with the assumptions of modern evolutionary science, which asserted the unity of nature as a realm dominated not by a divine plan but by immanent natural laws. At the age of sixteen, Kafka read Darwin's *The Origin of Species* and Haeckel's *The Riddles of the Universe*. Ernst Haeckel was one of the chief exponents of Darwinism in Germany, grafting it onto a well-established body of evolutionary assumptions that went back to the Romantic alliance between science and philosophy. These assumptions were shared with Nietzsche, who polemicized against Darwin's particular version of evolutionism. Nietzsche maintained that the motor driving evolution was not the individual's relation with its environment but an innate will to power which set one organism in conflict with another. While Haeckel

German evolutionary biologist Ernst Haeckel (1834–1919), shown here in a photograph from ca. 1918 (top), published *Die Welträtsel* (*The Riddles of the Universe*) in 1895–99. His version of evolutionary theory was mild and progressivist, in contrast to that of German philosopher Friedrich Nietzsche (1844–1900), shown here in a photograph taken ca. 1875 (bottom), who emphasized struggle and conflict. Nietzsche published *The Genealogy of Morals* in 1887.

gave a relatively mild, progressivist version of evolutionary theory, Nietzsche emphasized conflict, struggle, and mastery. Nietzsche also explores the consequences of evolutionary monism: if the physical universe is a single unit, there can be no categorical division between humanity and the rest of nature. Man is just another animal. He differs from the others in being fluid, malleable, imperfectly adapted to his environment, and hence without the health that characterizes all other animals:

> For man is more sick, more uncertain, more mutable, less defined than any other animal, there is no doubt about that—he is the sick animal. (*The Genealogy of Morals*, III 13; emphasis in original)

Second, Bucephalus is a survivor from a more heroic past. In "the present order of society" there is no room for heroes. Only the base or commonplace aspects of the heroic age have survived, like "the skill required to spear a friend across the banqueting table," as Alexander did his friend Cleitus, and the wish to escape from Macedonia (Alexander's kingdom, here used in a half-metaphorical way). This historical pessimism is an increasingly frequent motif in Kafka. At the end of "A Country Doctor," the doctor is alone and unprotected in a desolate snow-covered landscape, "naked, exposed to the frost of this unhappiest of ages." We hear repeatedly of decline: in "A Fasting Artist," the great age of starvation artists is past; in "Investigations of a Dog," the dogs have forgotten the true world they once knew; and the story *In the Penal Colony* shows the Officer recalling a glorious past under the Old Commandant.

Alexander killed Cleitus, his friend and an officer in the Macedonian army, during an argument. *The Murder of Cleitus* (1898–99), shown here, is by French illustrator Andre Castaigne.

Third, Alexander the Great is missed because, though his personal greatness was flawed, he could at least give a clear direction to reality by pointing his sword at the gates of India. The "gates of India" are here a metaphor for another reality, beyond and outside our familiar world. Nowadays we do not know even where to look for it. In a democratic age, many people try to assume Alexander's leadership role by pointing their swords, but they cannot agree where to point and only wave their swords about aimlessly, presenting a spectacle which the eye cannot take in— "the eye that tries to follow them grows confused." As in "The Passenger," the modern world provides no steady point of reference.

In representing Dr. Bucephalus as unrepresentable, Kafka intimates a deep skepticism about whether words can ever represent the world, whether art can express the truth. "Art flies round the truth, determined not to get burnt," runs one of his aphorisms. His skepticism finds expression in the little story "The Top."

· · · · ·

THE TOP

A philosopher always hung about where children were playing. And as soon as he spotted a boy with a top, he lay in wait. Scarcely had the top begun to spin than the philosopher would follow it in order to catch it. He was not troubled by the children's shouts and their attempts to keep him away from their toy; if he caught the top while it was still spinning, he was happy, but only for a moment, then he would throw it onto the ground and go away. For he believed that the knowledge of any detail, such as a spinning top, would suffice for knowledge of the universal. Therefore he did not spend his time with the great problems: that struck him as uneconomical. If the tiniest detail could really be known, then everything would be known, and therefore he spent his time only with the spinning top. And whenever the preparations had been made for spinning the top, he hoped it would now work, and when the top was spinning, he ran after it breathlessly, his hope became certainty, but when he held the stupid piece of wood in his hand, he would feel sick, and the shouting of the children, which he had not heard before and which now suddenly assailed his ears, chased him away, he reeled like a top spun by an unskillful whip.

· · · · ·

The philosopher seeks knowledge of the world. The tiniest part of the world will suffice to give him knowledge of the whole. The trouble is, the world does not stand still. It is in constant motion, like the spinning top, and will not stop for the philosopher to scrutinize it. If you stop the world, as the philosopher does the top, it no longer tells you anything. So the philosopher can never obtain the knowledge he seeks, and is driven away by the children, who with their noise and play are closer to ever-moving life than he is.

Kafka's Verbal Art

As these examples show, Kafka was an artist in words, and his texts need careful reading. Reading them in translation is like seeing a painting reproduced in black and white. Translation inevitably obscures key words that gather associations each time they recur. One such word, already mentioned, is *Verkehr*, which occurs at significant points in *The Judgment*. We are first told that Georg Bendemann's friend in Russia has "*keinen gesellschaftlichen Verkehr*" (no social intercourse) with the locals. Later we learn that Georg has not needed to go to his father's room for months, "*denn er verkehrte mit seinem Vater ständig im Geschäft*" (for he had constant dealings with his father in the business). This implies that Georg's "dealings" with his father are no different from his social and business contacts, makes him sound cold, and begins to erode the contrast previously implied between the sociable Georg and his isolated friend. Finally, as he falls to his death, "*ein geradezu unendlicher Verkehr*" crosses the bridge. Here "*Verkehr*" primarily means "traffic"; accumulating references to Georg's sexual greed make one think of another possible meaning, "sexual intercourse"; and from its previous occurrences it has acquired the implication of a whole world of social intercourse from which Georg is excluded, by his death and earlier perhaps by his egotism.

Though Kafka rewards close reading, critics have sometimes tried to use his wordplay as a crude key to his meaning, or have imagined wordplay that is not there. A cliché of Kafka interpretation finds puns in such words as *Verfahren*, which in *The Trial* has its usual sense of "legal procedure," but which is supposed also to suggest *ver-fahren*, "to go awry." In *The Castle*, K.'s profession of land surveyor (*Landvermesser*) is said also to suggest *Vermessenheit*, "presumption." However, these are at most potential puns. Kafka does nothing to call them to the reader's attention. I suspect that the critics who discern them are familiar with the etymologizing practiced by the philosopher Heidegger, who loved to extract new meaning from German words by separating their components (for example *er-innern*, "to remember," suggests also "to internalize"), and that they have mistakenly attributed this technique also to Kafka.

Likewise, there has been much speculation about characters' names. Kafka himself noted that "Bende-" and "Samsa" had the same pattern of vowels and consonants as "Kafka." Given Kafka's knowledge of Czech, it is tempting to associate Samsa with the Czech *sám*, "oneself"; Klamm in *The Castle* with *klam*, "illusion"; and Lasemann with *lázen*, "bath," though these meanings only reinforce what the text already conveys. Names taken from the classics (Momus) or the Bible (Galater, a Castle official whose name comes from St. Paul's epistle to the Galatians) have encouraged elaborate but inconclusive interpretations. Some may just be jokes. Momus was the Greek god of mirth; but when Kafka's Momus solemnly announces his name, "everyone suddenly became very serious." There is certainly a vulgar joke in *The Trial* in the name Fräulein Bürstner, which can be rendered in English as "Miss Scrubber."

Finally, Kafka indulges in private allusions, which the reader need not understand. Knowing that his surname meant "jackdaw" (*kavka* in Czech), he introduces many allusions to jackdaws, crows, and ravens. The hero of the early fragment *Wedding Preparations in the Country* is called Eduard Raban (German *Rabe*, "raven"). The hunter Gracchus, who has been trapped between life and death since the fourth century, bears the name of a famous Roman family meaning "jackdaw." When K. first glimpses the Castle, it is surrounded by crows.

Even when plausible, these allusions do little to help us understand Kafka's texts. Critics who rely on them often seem to want a key which will give immediate access to Kafka's texts without needing to read and appreciate Kafka's written words. They seek to decode Kafka's texts rather than to understand them. Understanding should be envisaged, not as the discovery of a meaning which can be summed up in a sentence, but rather as Conrad describes Marlow's stories in *Heart of Darkness* (1902): "to him the meaning of an episode was not inside like a kernel but outside, enveloping the tale which brought it out only as a glow brings out a haze."

Some of Kafka's work is incomplete. He was dissatisfied with his three novels because they were unfinished. But they are incomplete in different ways. In *The Man Who Disappeared* the action breaks down into episodes, the most substantial being the "Theatre of Oklahoma" chapter (Kafka spelled it "Oklahama"). With *The Trial*, Kafka, knowing his tendency to digress, began by writing the first and last chapters, dealing with Josef K.'s arrest and his execution, and then wrote the rest, putting each chapter into a folder and indicating its contents but not its place in the sequence. Several chapters are unfinished, some of them incompatible with the action in the main body of the novel. English translations of *The Trial* that omit these fragmentary chapters make the novel seem more coherent than it really is. The order even of the completed chapters cannot be finally determined because the available indications contradict one another. *The Castle*, by contrast, has a continuous, though very expansive, narrative line, but does not reach a clear conclusion. Kafka was not content to leave his novels as fragments. He regarded them as failures. There is no reason to doubt Kafka's sincerity in instructing Brod to burn them, but if Brod had obeyed, instead of publishing them and taking the manuscripts with him on the last train to leave Prague before the Nazi occupation of Czechoslovakia in 1939, twentieth-century literature would look very different.

Kafka relies on hints and suggestions. In revising *The Castle*, he excised sentences that showed K. clearly aware of his own motives. Thus Kafka originally made K. perceive the futility of his conflict with the Castle by reflecting: "In this way I was fighting not the others but rather myself." Going over the manuscript, however, Kafka deleted this sentence, leaving this conclusion to be drawn by the reader and thus, as usual in modernist literature, assigning the reader a more active role.

The reader of Kafka often catches characters betraying themselves out of their own mouths. Thus the Village Mayor in *The Castle* explains to K. that though he has been summoned as a land surveyor when the

Brod escaped Prague with Kafka's papers just before the Nazi occupation of Czechoslovakia. Adolf Hitler, in an open car, is shown being greeted by Sudeten Germans in the north of Czechoslovakia in 1938.

village has no need for one, this may be a misunderstanding, but it can scarcely be an error. The excellent organization of the Castle bureaucracy does not allow for the possibility of error. The authorities have "control authorities" to monitor their work.

> Are there control authorities? There are nothing but control authorities. Of course, their purpose is not to uncover errors in the ordinary meaning of the word, since errors do not occur and even when an error does in fact occur, as in your case, who can say conclusively that it is an error?

Moreover, since each control bureau is monitored by others, the first may acknowledge an error, but who is to say that the second control bureaux will form the same judgment and then the third and subsequently the others?

We have a picture of innumerable offices so busy monitoring one another that no actual work gets done.

In *The Trial*, the Advocate explains to his client Josef K. that the Court does not admit defense lawyers to its hearings, but denies that this makes defense lawyers redundant:

> The aim was to eliminate all defense, the accused man must be left to his own devices. Basically not a bad principle, but nothing would be more mistaken than to infer from this that advocates for the defense were not necessary at this court.

When Josef K.'s landlady says she thinks his arrest is "something scholarly," K. hastens to agree with her, but in doing so he twists her words:

> I too share your opinion to some extent, but I judge the whole thing more strictly than you and I consider it to be not even scholarly but nothing at all.

In these cases, the illogic is not just intellectual folly: it is increasingly self-serving. The Village Mayor cannot admit the fallibility of the authorities on whom his position depends; the Advocate wants to gain power over clients, even though he can do nothing for them; and Josef K., in denying that his arrest means anything, is repressing his latent sense of guilt.

The above examples also illustrate Kafka's humor, something for which he receives too little credit. Sometimes, as here, his humor consists in the exposure of self-serving illogic. Sometimes it circles around a paradox, as in the description of the indescribable Bucephalus. Kafka's love of paradox often issues in wit; most devastatingly, on his deathbed he asked for euthanasia, saying: "If you don't kill me, you're a murderer." Sometimes Kafka exploits the figure of regress, as when the Village Mayor asserts that not only are the authorities monitored; the authorities do nothing but monitor one another; or in the diary entry in which Kafka, feeling he has to build up his life from the beginning, compares himself to a theater director:

> A theater director who has to create everything from scratch, he even has to father the actors. A visitor is denied admittance on the grounds that the director is engaged in important theater business. What is it? He is changing the nappies on a future actor.

Often his humor takes the form of the gratuitously specific detail, as when Gregor Samsa recalls his love life:

> a chambermaid in one of the provincial hotels—a sweet and fleeting memory—, a cashier in a hat shop, whose affections he had earnestly but too leisurely courted.

Kafka also has some knockabout humor, as in Karl's misadventures in *The Man Who Disappeared*, the antics of the assistants in *The Castle*, or the first chapter of *The Trial*, in which the guards keep bumping into the increasingly flustered Josef K. as he searches for his papers and can find at first only a bicycle license. Max Brod reports that when Kafka read this chapter aloud, he and his listeners were convulsed with laughter, and if one reads it as the discomfiture of a pompous official, it is not hard to understand this reaction.

However, *Humor* (humor) in German denotes neither comedy nor wit, but a resigned acceptance of life's imperfections. Such a gentle, playful humor pervades Kafka's letters, especially those to Brod and other male friends, and is frequent also in his tales. Thus in "A Problem for the Father of the Family," the narrator is mildly worried about the mysterious creature named Odradek who haunts his house, laughing with "the sort of laughter that can be produced without lungs [. . .] like the rustling of fallen leaves." Here, as so often, humor comes at the expense of the humorless. Just as the stuffy Josef K. and the authoritarian K. are discomposed by the two guards and the two assistants, so the conventional father of the family is worried by having a being in his house for whom he cannot account. A story Kafka never published, "Blumfeld, an Elderly Bachelor," shows the lonely, grouchy Blumfeld being disconcerted one evening when he returns from work to his normally empty flat and finds it occupied by two celluloid balls that persist in bouncing. In order to get some sleep, Blumfeld has to trap them in his wardrobe. Although the story is incomplete, one can discern some connection between the two balls and the two irrepressible clerks in Blumfeld's office who keep larking about despite his scowls. In all these cases, humor comes from the reluctance of the main character to admit something alien into his life.

A related type of humor comes from a change of perspective. From the perspective of the Court, Josef K. is far less important than he is in his own eyes. He is even asked, humiliatingly, whether he is an interior decorator, to which he replies with indignation: "No, I am senior administrator in a large bank," thus provoking inexplicable laughter. In Kafka's last story, "Josefine, the Songstress or: The Mouse People," the pretensions of an artist (of *the* artist?) are satirized by a reflective narrator who broods over the paradox that the admired singer Josefine does not sing but only squeaks like all the other mice. Though she thinks herself the savior of her people, she is only the mouthpiece through which the spirit of the mouse nation reaches each individual. "May Josefine be spared the awareness that the fact that we listen to her is a proof that she is no true singer," concludes the narrator, revealing a perspective from which the would-be artist Josefine is self-deluded, childish, and indulged by the generosity of her fellow mice. The narrator's grave humor thus gradually strips away Josefine's pretensions. This strange mixture of gentle humor, relentless questioning, and sadness forms an emotional tone much more characteristic of Kafka than the horror and bafflement usually associated with the term *Kafkaesque*. Through his humor, Kafka has introduced a new tone into literature, like a new mixture of colors or a new musical note.

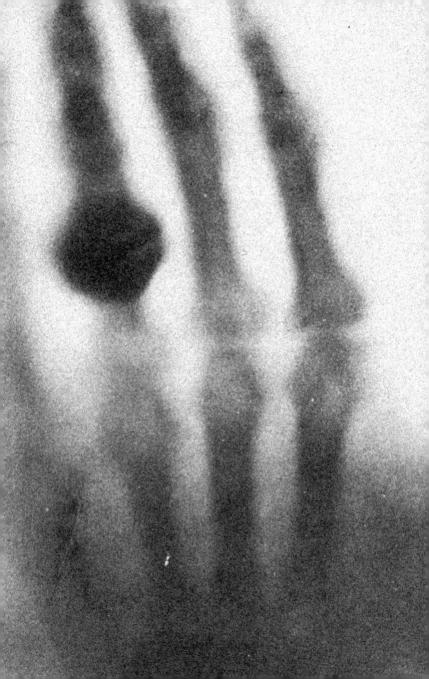

THREE

Bodies

●

The Modern Body

"When Gregor Samsa awoke one morning from troubled dreams he found himself transformed in his bed into a monstrous insect." This must be Kafka's most famous sentence. But, like many Kafka sentences, it is full of puzzles. Gregor's body is transformed, but his mind remains human: is "himself" synonymous with his body, as opposed to his mind? And Gregor does not exactly "find" himself transformed: rather, although he sees his brown belly and numerous legs, he fails to register this incomprehensible fact. After briefly wondering "What has happened to me?" he reverts to the consciousness of

---

Kafka shared the modern sensibility that accepts the body's death, as exemplified by Thomas Mann's protagonist Hans Castorp, who when he sees an X-ray of his own hand becomes alienated from his body and is able to accept his mortality.

a busy commercial traveler who has to get up early on a wet morning to catch the five o'clock train.

By inserting the mind of a harassed employee into the body of a huge insect, Kafka has dramatized the division between the mind and the body which is a central theme of Western culture. Building on the long-standing Christian dualism of soul and body, the philosophical tradition of rationalism, whose best-known landmark is Descartes, distinguished sharply between the mind, the disembodied site of reason, and the body, the domain of sensations and feelings. The body had to be subordinated to the mind, reshaped by an intellectual discipline, and feeling had to be subject to reason. The authority of the mind over the body was external-ized by clothes: by the stiff collars that forced the Victorian man to keep his head firmly upright, and the corsets that constrained his wife's body. In the late nineteenth century, however, the body found its philosophical spokesman in Nietzsche, whose work the younger generation throughout Europe, including Kafka, read avidly from the 1890s onwards. In his pro-phetic book *Thus Spoke Zarathustra* (1884), Nietzsche proclaimed that the faculty known as mind or intelligence was merely a small part of the great, instinctive intelligence residing in the body (see sidebar).

Following Nietzsche's summons, much modern literature explores our bodily existence. The greatest such undertaking is Thomas Mann's *The Magic Mountain* (1924), an epic of illness, in which Hans Castorp explores, among much else, the wonders of medical science during his seven-year stay in a Swiss sanatorium. Allowed to see the X-ray image of his own hand, he is at once alienated from his own body, seeing it as a skeleton whose flesh has been dissolved away, and reconciled to it, for the sight convinces him that he will die and enables him to accept his own mortality.

· · · · ·

OF THE DESPISERS OF THE BODY

I wish to speak to the despisers of the body. Let them not learn differently nor teach differently, but only bid farewell to their own bodies—and so become dumb.

"I am body and soul"—so speaks the child. And why should one not speak like children?

But the awakened, the enlightened man says: I am body entirely, and nothing beside; and soul is only a word for something in the body.

The body is a great intelligence, a multiplicity with one sense, a war and a peace, a herd and a herdsman.

Your little intelligence, my brother, which you call "spirit," is also an instrument of your body, a little instrument and toy of your great intelligence.

You say "I" and you are proud of this word. But greater than this—although you will not believe in it—is your body and its great intelligence, which does not say "I" but performs "I."

Nietzsche, Thus Spoke Zarathustra, *tr. R. J. Hollingdale (Harmondsworth:*
Penguin, 1961)

· · · · ·

German author Thomas Mann, who won the Nobel Prize for Literature in 1929, published *Der Zauberberg* (*The Magic Mountain*) in 1924. The first-edition title page of the popular novel, which explores humanity's bodily existence (among much else), is shown here.

The modern sensibility that Kafka shares, however, not only accepts the body's death but, by so doing, finds new value in the body's life. Many of Kafka's contemporaries opposed the nineteenth-century tendency to conceal the body under layers of clothing and distort its shape by corsetry. They advocated the frank and unashamed acceptance of the naked body as genuine and natural. The nudity of Greek sculpture need not be confined to museums but could be a practical ideal for modern man, though the modern body should not have the whiteness of marble but be bronzed by the sun. Nudism, though only possible in limited spaces, was presented as the highest form of healthy living. Reformers also recommended practical and comfortable clothing that allowed the body to breathe, and urged people to flee from insanitary cities to specially designed garden suburbs like Hellerau near Dresden (where Kafka's sister Elli considered sending her son to a progressive school). The cult of the natural also inspired the Wandervogel movement, by virtue of which thousands of young men and women went hiking through Germany, sleeping in the open air. Kafka himself was keen on rowing, swimming, and hiking. His friend Brod recalls:

Kafka and I were keen hikers. Every Sunday, often Saturdays as well, we were in the forests surrounding Prague whose beauty encouraged a cult of innocence and enthusiasm. [. . .] We swam in the forest streams, for Kafka and I lived then in the strange belief that we had not possessed a countryside until a nearly physical bond had been forged by swimming in its living, streaming waters. (Max Brod, *Streitbares Leben*, quoted in Mark Anderson, *Kafka's Clothes* [Oxford: Clarendon Press, 1992], p. 76)

Kafka did gymnastic exercises twice daily, naked, in front of an open window. He urged his fiancée Felice to exercise as well, and to learn to swim. In his pursuit of healthy living he became a vegetarian (something far more eccentric then than it is now), and even followed a special method of chewing his food known as *"fletschern"* after its American propagator Horace Fletcher. In the summer of 1912 Kafka spent two weeks at the nudist colony Jungborn in the Harz Mountains in Germany. At Jungborn, nudity was part of a program of physical and spiritual renewal, with group exercises, lectures on vegetarianism and clothing reform, and open-air Christian religious services. Harmony was sought between the body and the soul. In its program of renewal through the body, the Jungborn colony anticipated the cult of the body that spread across Europe in the 1920s and is now central to modern culture. Throughout North America and Western Europe, it has been argued, the care of the body through dieting and sunbathing has replaced the attention formerly given to the soul, and regular workouts at the gym or health club occupy the ritual space vacated by the practice of churchgoing.

In Kafka's case, however, this physical activity does not indicate an untroubled acceptance of his body. It is one side of a deep ambivalence. The other side finds expression in constant complaints in his diary about his thin, unhealthy body, which he fears is too long for his weak heart to be able to pump blood through it. Some alarming diary entries imagine a hideous punishment being inflicted on his body. Thus on May 4, 1913, he compulsively imagines the kind of circular blade that cuts meat into strips rapidly slicing into his body. A letter he wrote to Milena in September 1920 is illustrated with a picture of a man tied by his hands and feet to two poles which are being moved so as to tear him apart. If for Kafka the body is capable of redemption through healthy living, it is also the supreme site of punishment.

Gregor's transformation into an insect drastically expresses Kafka's ambivalence toward his body and toward the body in general. His transformation and his failure to notice it convey the degree to which Gregor is alienated from his own body. He has to cope with the concrete task of getting a large and unwieldy insect body out of bed, still believing that he must and will catch his train. His obsession with his job reveals the self-estrangement imposed on him by its demands. "That boy thinks of nothing but his work," his mother assures the chief clerk of Gregor's firm, who, exercising an implausibly but alarmingly thorough surveillance, has come to see why he wasn't at the station. Even so, mind and body are linked by the language of the unconscious, which can involuntarily reveal the truth. Still lying in bed, Gregor reflects that one of his colleagues is "a mere creature [*Kreatur*] of the chief, spineless and stupid." The word *spineless* betrays Gregor's unconscious awareness that he himself is now an invertebrate. This commerce between the body and the unconscious mind blurs the contrast between Gregor's human mind and animal body.

As Gregor struggles out of bed, Kafka recounts his maneuvers in a minutely detailed, deadpan style, ironically mimicking how Gregor concentrates on the immediate task as a way of repressing awareness of his grotesque situation. But, since Kafka's prose is always surrounded by a penumbra of further suggestion, Gregor's laborious antics—getting upright by clinging to the wardrobe, leaning on the back of a chair and pushing it toward the door—may evoke the experience of someone unexpectedly disabled who has to use the body in new ways to perform previously straightforward tasks. And Gregor's new physicality makes him more exposed to pain. Not only does he hurt his head in falling out of bed, but when he unlocks the door by turning the key with his jaws, he injures himself in a way that causes a brown fluid to drip from his mouth. However much he may endorse the modern ideal of the healthy body, Kafka keeps reminding us that the body is also fragile and vulnerable.

Other characters too are presented in bodily terms. We first encounter Gregor's father, mother, and sister as they knock at the three doors of his bedroom, urging him to get up. When he emerges from his room, their reactions, and that of the chief clerk, are conveyed by gestures. The chief clerk, putting his hand to his open mouth, "started slowly backing away, as if he were being driven by the steady pressure of some invisible force," while Gregor's mother faints, and:

> his father clenched a fist with a menacing expression, as if he meant to beat Gregor back to his room, then he looked uncertainly round the living-room, covered his eyes with his hands and fell into a sobbing that shook his mighty chest.

As here, Kafka frequently describes people through gesture and expression, often leaving it obscure what the gestures and expressions actually mean. In his fiction, people's bodies are opaque, in need of an interpretation that can never be conclusive. The "as if" formulation illustrated here may well have been encouraged by Kafka's reading of Dickens. But what in Dickens was a device for humorous exaggeration has in Kafka become a basic means of representing the inscrutable world of other people. Insofar as other people can be understood at all, it is through their bodily self-expression.

The hints of violence in the just-quoted description of Gregor's father are fulfilled later. The second time Gregor leaves his room, he finds that his father has also been transformed: not from a human into an insect, but from a decrepit old man into a vigorous, upright one, with bushy eyebrows, well-combed hair, and sharp eyes. Advancing toward Gregor, he lifts his feet high, astonishing Gregor with "the gigantic size of the soles of his boots," and suggesting to the reader that he may squash Gregor like an ordinary insect. Instead, his father drives Gregor back to his room by bombarding him with apples from the fruit bowl, one of which lodges in his back, causing him "shocking, unbelievable pain." Eventually the apple becomes the center of a festering wound that contributes to Gregor's death.

The Gendered Body

The body's potential for violence is closely linked, here and elsewhere in Kafka, to sexuality. A hard-pressed commercial traveler, obliged to support his parents and sister, Gregor's sexual life has been limited to a few brief encounters and to the pinup that hangs opposite his bed, showing "a lady complete with fur hat and fur stole, who was sitting upright and extending to view a thick fur muff into which the whole of her forearm had vanished." Clearly Kafka kept an eye on the fashion magazines, for such fur costumes were especially in vogue in autumn 1912, when Kafka wrote this story. The blatant sexuality of this image, enhanced by the hint of coition in the description, lets us guess what Gregor's "troubled dreams" were about, and suggest too that the "mass of little white spots which he was unable to interpret" covering his belly may result from a nocturnal emission.

The costume worn by the woman in the pinup on Gregor Samsa's wall was wearing the height of fashion, as shown by this magazine cover from less than a year earlier.

Kafka's bodies are gendered, not just in the banal sense that some are male and others female, but also in that certain cultural behaviors are associated with male bodies, others with female bodies, and thus are coded as masculine or feminine. The masculine body in Kafka is firm, upright, soldierly, like the body of Herr Samsa after his seeming rejuvenation, or like the body of Herr Bendemann when he leaps upright to confront his cowering son. Josef K. blustering to an assembly and K. in *The Castle* assaulting his assistant with his stick similarly show masculine authoritarianism. This masculinity is often supported by a tight uniform, like Herr Samsa's "tight-fitting blue uniform with gilt buttons," the heavy military uniform of the Officer from *In the Penal Colony*, or the uncomfortably stiff uniform into which the unfortunate

Karl Rossmann is thrust when working as a lift-boy in *The Man Who Disappeared*. While the uniform insulates the masculine body from nature, the feminine body is coded as natural by its animal traits, as with the lady in furs, or Leni, the Advocate's housekeeper in *The Trial*—like a strange evolutionary throwback, Leni has webs between her fingers, and K. says of her hand: "What a pretty claw!" The feminine body may also be defined by its sheer bulk. Brunelda in *The Man Who Disappeared* is a mass of flesh, unable to walk downstairs without support. Her description recalls a diary entry (July 23, 1913) conveying Kafka's fascinated disgust with women's bodies, their "exploding sexuality" and "natural uncleanliness."

Bodies in Kafka's fiction, however, cross gender boundaries. Some women become masculinized as hypersexual, threatening figures, like the lady in furs, the athletic Klara in *The Man Who Disappeared*, or Gregor's sister, who increasingly threatens her insect-brother with her fist. Men, conversely, are feminized. Georg is reduced to passive obedience before his father. Gregor exchanges the upright masculine posture for a horizontal posture, crawling on the floor, like the degraded prisoner from *In the Penal Colony* who crawls on all fours like a dog, or Josef K. as he lies down to be executed "like a dog." Not only does Gregor lie flat, like his mother when she faints, but he is further feminized by acquiring a large curved belly, like a pregnant woman. A fantasy of becoming a woman is also suggested when he expresses envy for his colleagues who "live like harem women." In later texts, the protagonist's masculinity is eroded more relentlessly by a process of bodily attrition. Josef K. pursuing his case, and K. trying to reach the Castle, succumb to ever-increasing exhaustion. Josef K.'s weariness is expressed by his gestures:

But instead of working he shuffled about in his chair, slowly pushed some objects around on his desk, and then, without being conscious of it, left his arm outstretched on the desktop and sat motionless with his head bowed.

The bowed head expresses submission, as it did when Josef K. earlier saw other litigants sitting in a row with bowed heads and bent backs. K., similarly, manages to reach an official's room, only to fall asleep on the bed and miss the message the official is giving him.

Kafka's feminized men lose out in an Oedipal struggle with father figures. Josef K. is easily seduced away from pursuing his case, and futilely plans to avenge himself on the Examining Magistrate by taking away the latter's mistress. K. envies the sexual potency ascribed to Castle officials, especially Klamm, who is said to be desired by all the village women. And in *The Transformation*, active sexuality is the domain of the parents, from which Gregor is excluded. Just before he loses consciousness from the pain caused by the apple his father throws at him, he almost witnesses a primal scene:

> With his last conscious look he saw the door of his room being flung open and his mother rushing out ahead of his screaming sister; in her chemise, for his sister had taken off her dress to help her breathe when she fainted; he saw his mother running toward his father, shedding her loosened petticoats one by one on the floor behind her; and how she stumbled over her skirts to fling herself upon him, and embraced him, quite united with him—but here Gregor's sight went dim—imploring him, with her hands clasped round his father's neck, to spare Gregor's life.

Gregor's sight goes dim to prevent him seeing what he must not see, an act of parental coition which, in sparing his life, re-enacts the one that gave him life. But his own sexuality reappears later when, hearing his sister play the violin, he fantasizes about inviting her into his room, keeping her there permanently, and kissing her on her bare neck. Under pressure from unconscious desire, his language becomes illogical:

> He would never let her out of his room again, at least not for so long as he lived; his terrible shape would be of service to him for the first time; at every door of his room he would stand guard at once, hissing and spitting at all intruders; his sister, however, should not be forced to stay with him, but should do so freely.

Here and elsewhere in Kafka, bodily desire reduces the mind to incoherence, illustrating the sway of the body's "great intelligence," as Nietzsche called it, over the small and powerless intellect lodged in the brain.

In some ways Gregor's transformation is liberating. It frees him from the tyranny of a demanding job and from the constraints of logic and rationality. It brings him closer to a precultural state of self-gratification. If the Enlightenment set up the "noble savage" as the imagined ideal antithesis to civilized humanity, the twentieth century, debarred by the colonization of the globe from fantasizing about primitive peoples, replaced this image with that of the young child, supposed by Freud to be a totally sexualized being for whom all physical contact is a source of sexual pleasure. Gregor does not reach this Utopia, but when confined to his room he does manage to enjoy himself. With the sticky pads on his feet, he crawls over the walls and ceiling of his room and falls onto the floor or sofa without hurting himself. This relative freedom from gravity represents a fantasy often indulged in Kafka's fiction. We have the trapeze artist of "First Sorrow," who spends all his time, except when traveling, aloft on his trapeze; the speaker who escapes from wartime fuel shortages by sitting astride a coal scuttle and ascending "into the regions of the ice mountains," never to be seen again; and the fantasy of endless, autonomous movement formulated in the early sketch "Longing to Be a Red Indian."

· · · · ·

LONGING TO BE A RED INDIAN

Oh to be a Red Indian, instantly prepared, and astride one's galloping mount, leaning into the wind, to skim with each fleeting quivering touch over the quivering ground, till one shed the spurs, for there were no spurs, till one flung off the reins, for there were no reins, and could barely see the land unfurl as a smooth-shorn heath before one, now that horse's neck and horse's head were gone.

· · · · ·

Another, more questionable liberation that Gregor experiences is from eating. Once his family have accepted his transformation, they wonder how to feed him. For some time Gregor eats food that humans find disgusting. He eagerly consumes a cheese which the day before, in human form, he had declared to be moldy. But soon he loses his appetite for any available food, and survives without eating, like an ascetic or an anorexic. His appetite becomes a desire for something unknown and unattainable. It is aroused when he hears his sister playing the violin to entertain the three lodgers as they eat a hearty dinner of meat and potatoes: "'I've got appetite enough,' said Gregor sadly to himself, 'but not for things of that kind. How these lodgers feed themselves up, while I waste away!'" The lodgers show no appreciation of the music, yet for Gregor it seems to point toward an unknown source of satisfaction: "Was he an animal, that music could move him so? It seemed to him as if the way were opening toward the unknown nourishment he craved." By a strange paradox, music, the most disembodied of the arts (and one that Gregor did not appreciate before his transformation), seems now to be pointing him toward a source of nourishment—perhaps an equally bodiless, spiritual nourishment, contrasting with the meat on which the lodgers gorge themselves?

Fasting

Fasting is central to Kafka's imagination. As a means of abandoning the physical world, and possibly entering a spiritual one, it fascinated Kafka, but also aroused his skepticism. Its supreme exponent in his writings is the Fasting Artist, whose superhuman powers of starvation are displayed to the public at fairs. There was a real fashion for such gruesome displays. In 1880 the American Henry Tanner undertook to starve for forty days in New York's Clarendon Hall for the edification of visitors who each paid twenty cents to see him. He accomplished this feat without apparent ill effects. The most famous starvation artist was Giovanni Succi, who performed in all Europe's major cities, with a team of farmers watching in case he nibbled on the sly. The Viennese author Peter Altenberg reports on a female starvation artist who fasted in a glass box under constant surveillance. Interest in such feats of emaciation did decline, as Kafka says, though the fashion seems to be returning: as I write, an American "magician" is suspended in a glass case above Tower Bridge in London, resolved to starve publicly for forty-four days. Kafka's Fasting Artist is dedicated

SUCCI'S LONG FAST.

THE ITALIAN SAYS THAT HE WILL GO WITHOUT FOOD FOR 45 DAYS.

Signor Giovanni Succi, an Italian gentleman who has attained some fame as a professional faster, began last night what he declares will be a forty-five days' fast. Persons who would like to see how he fasts can find him in the small hall over Koster & Bial's place of entertainment, in West Twenty-third Street, at any hour of the day or night. A section of the hall has been marked off by a railing, and within that section are a bed, lounge, tables, and chairs for the use of Signor Succi.

The faster dined there last evening in the presence of a score or more of ladies and gentlemen, and his repast consisted of anchovies, boiled trout, olives, celery, risotta, (an Italian baked dish comprising rice, mushrooms, cheese, and wine,) cauliflower, kidney stew, roast chicken, roast partridge, roast quail, grapes, pears, and a quart bottle of Chianti. It took Succi about an hour to clear the cloth, and he left few fragments. At 8:10 o'clock he lighted a cigar and began to fast. He was then weighed and measured by a committee of physicians, comprised of Dr. G. Bettini Di Moise, his personal physician, and Drs. Frank H. Ingram, Henry V. Wildman, Edwin Gaillard Mason, M. W. Lynde, and Hugh Hagan, all of this city.

This *New York Times* article from November 6, 1890, profiles the Italian professional faster Giovanni Succi.

to his art and frustrated by the compromises with public taste forced on him by his manager, who will never allow him to starve for more than forty days. Only after the public has lost interest in such feats is the Fasting Artist able to starve for as long as he likes, yet his prodigies of starving are unrecorded and unrecognized. On his deathbed, he confesses to the overseer that his fasting deserves no admiration: he could not help doing it,

because I could never find the nourishment I liked. Had I found
it, believe me, I would never have caused any stir, and would have
eaten my fill just like you and everyone else.

So apparently it is not a vocation, but simply a distaste for ordinary
living, that made him into an artist. Or is that just the self-deprecation
forced on him by his too-tender artistic conscience?

Refusing to eat places one outside the ordinary bestial world in
which life feeds on other lives. Kafka figures this world by the image
of the panther, which proves far more popular as a circus attraction
than the starvation artist. Visitors flock to see it, almost overwhelmed
by "the joy of life [that] glowed so fiercely from the furnace of its
throat." This is life as Nietzsche and his readers understood it: "A
living thing wants above all else to release its strength; life itself is the
will to power," wrote Nietzsche in *Beyond Good and Evil*; and in *The
Genealogy of Morals*, "life operates essentially—that is, in terms of its
basic functions—through injury, violation, exploitation, and destruction, and cannot be conceived in any other way." Gregor's family
too can be violent and coercive when their interests are threatened.
Once Gregor is dead, his father ejects the lodgers from the family
flat, and as the lodgers trail down the stairs, up comes a butcher's boy
carrying a tray of meat—the antithesis to the starved Gregor. The
guards who ensure that the Fasting Artist does not eat on the sly are
also butchers. To celebrate their liberation from Gregor's presence, all
three family members take the day off work and go out to the country.
Admiring their daughter, the Samsa parents decide that it is time to
find a husband for her, and their intentions seem confirmed when,
at the end of their tram journey, she rises and stretches her young

body—anticipating the physical grace of the panther. The panther, with its predatory energy, is a better image of life than the ascetic, life-denying artist. It is only the fastidious modern pessimist, according to Nietzsche, who finds life "distasteful."

Kafka, however, takes the side of the ascetic, contrasting his self-starving with the untroubled appetites of flesh eaters. In "Investigations of a Dog," the narrator dog separates himself from the canine community and starves in the hope of discovering where the dogs' food comes from. He is roused from his fast by a hunting dog who drives him away. In the novel set in America, *The Man Who Disappeared*, one of the hostile authority figures, Mr. Green, eats a huge dinner with undiminishing appetite, and censures the young protagonist Karl for not eating; later, Mr. Green's huge size makes Karl briefly wonder whether he may have eaten up another of the guests. In a variant passage of "A Fasting Artist," Kafka introduces an actual cannibal, an old friend of the Fasting Artist who pays him a visit. Besides his rough manners, the cannibal is distinguished by his huge shock of red hair: "The sight was not at all ridiculous, but was terrifying, as though this superhuman head of hair indicated superhuman appetites and the strength to satisfy them." When life is embodied in such brutes, the ascetic wish to die away from life becomes more understandable.

The physicality and sexuality repressed by Kafka's protagonists, usually busy professional men, returns in frightening or disgusting forms of which Gregor's insect guise is only the most drastic example. Both disgust and violence attend the animal imagery evoked in the story "A Country Doctor." The doctor has been summoned by a patient who lives ten miles away, but his horse has died: how can he get there? He accidentally kicks an abandoned pigsty, and it opens to reveal a stable, from which emerge two huge horses, "mighty creatures with powerful flanks [. . .] dipping their shapely heads like camels," and a groom who himself seems half-animal: he calls the horses "brother" and "sister"; he embraces the doctor's servant girl and bites her in the cheek, whereupon the doctor, threatening him with a whip, calls him "you brute." Breaking down doors in pursuit of his victim, the groom is another embodiment of physical life as will to power and appetite. The doctor, on the other hand, is not an ascetic, but a diminished person. He is conscientious, obsessed with his unrewarding job (he complains how hard he works for his ungrateful patients); his corporeality, his sexuality, has been banished, only to reemerge as disgusting and violent (the pigsty, *Schweinestall*, has strong connotations of filth [*Schweinerei*]). Until the emergence of the hypersexual groom, the doctor scarcely noticed his maidservant; initially he refers to her as "it" (Kafka is exploiting the fact that *Dienstmädchen*, "maidservant," is a neuter noun). Only after the groom names her as Rosa does the doctor also use her name. Thereafter he repeatedly and graphically imagines the groom's copulation with her, wishing he could "drag her out from under that groom." Once his sexuality has been aroused, it persists as a painful obsession.

Corporeality sometimes appears, as in this story, as a brutal and frightening irruption into a life that has become an unsatisfying routine. It can also appear as a wound, an image that preoccupies Kafka's imagination. Gregor is wounded, perhaps fatally, by his father, and we are told that "the apple remained embedded in his flesh as a visible reminder." A reminder of what? Given the story's Christian context (the Samsa parents cross themselves on learning of Gregor's death), it recalls the "thorn in the flesh" which afflicted St. Paul (2 Cor. 12:7) and which has often been read as a nagging reminder of sexuality. In the earlier story *The Judgment* the father bears the scar of a war wound on his thigh (the genital area). The ape in "A Report to an Academy," who claims to have become human, was wounded by the hunters who, when capturing him in Africa, shot him below the hip, so that he still limps. But the most remarkable wound is the one displayed by the boy to whom the Country Doctor has been summoned. At first the boy seems to have nothing wrong with him, and the doctor is about to chide him for malingering, when a whinny from the horses makes him look closer and see something which, if it were literally there, he could never have missed:

> On his right side, in the region of the hip, a wound has opened up as big as the palm of my hand. Rose-red, in various shades, dark in the depths, paler towards the edges, finely grained, with blood welling unevenly, open like a mine at the surface. Thus from the distance. A closer look reveals a further complication. Who can set his eyes on that without whistling softly? Worms, as thick and long as my little finger, rose-red themselves and blood-spattered in addition, held fast in the depths of the wound, are wriggling with their little white heads and their numerous legs towards the light. Poor boy, you are past helping. I have found your great wound, this flower in your side is destroying you.

Commentary can barely hint at the diverse and disturbing suggestions of this passage. Its situation "in the region of the hip" relates the wound, like other wounds in Kafka, to sexuality, as does its association with the maidservant Rosa. The minute care with which the wound's red shading is described, almost as though it were an aesthetic object, stands in contrast to its blatant sexual character. This impossibly huge, vaginal gash in the body incarnates the terrors associated by men with the female genitals. Like a mine shaft, it seems to open up the body of Mother Earth, and its blood suggests defloration and menstruation (assisted by the "blood-soaked handkerchief" the boy's sister is waving). The boy seems to have been castrated and feminized, perhaps rendered androgynous or removed from sexual differentiation.

Yet the wound also contains life. Many-legged worms (unknown to natural history) are wriggling in it, as though the boy's body were already decaying. And the wound, associated with roses, is now compared to a flower. In dying and decaying, the boy's body is also flowering into new life—a life conditional on the death of the body. Is this a reminder that we are organisms, whose reabsorption into the material universe will nourish future organisms? Or does it point to a reality quite different from material existence?

Often Kafka shows an inclination to reject bodily existence, especially insofar as it is sexual. His story "The Silence of the Sirens" (1917) retells the myth by explaining that it is not the song of the Sirens that is really dangerous, but their silence. Not knowing this, Odysseus stuffs wax in his ears and has himself tied to the mast. Although the Sirens keep silent, Odysseus observes "the twistings of their necks, their panting, their tear-filled eyes, their half-open mouths," but interprets this as the gestures accompanying song, not as the extravagant display of erotic desire. Thus, by a mere misunderstanding, he remains secure from the sexual temptations of the physical world. A day or two earlier, Kafka wrote in the same notebook a drastic portrayal of the physical world, under the heading "A Life":

A stinking bitch, bearer of many children, already rotting in places, but which was everything to me in my childhood, which incessantly follows me faithfully, which I cannot bring myself to strike and before which, avoiding her breath, I move back step by step, and which, if I don't make a different decision, will force me into the already visible angle of the wall, so that there she may completely decay on me and with me, to the last—does it honor me?—the pus- and worm-filled flesh of her tongue on my hand.

Just as the boy's wound was a flower devoured by worms, so fertility here accompanies decay. The dog is an embodiment of femininity, with its many puppies, its association with the speaker's childhood, and its overpowering affection which the speaker can hardly bear to resist, even though it seeks to drag him down into its own physical corruption. The speaker is tied to it, and thus to the world, by residual affection, by what used to be love. It is ultimately love that enslaves us to the sensual world, as Kafka soon afterward wrote in an aphorism: "Sensual love deceives one into ignoring heavenly love; it could not do so by itself, but as it unconsciously contains the element of heavenly love, it can." Sensual love is a version of heavenly love; it contains enough that is genuine to distract us effectively from seeking after heavenly love.

Reading Kafka's later stories and aphorisms, one sometimes feels strangely transported back to the world of early Christian and Jewish mystics and martyrs. The rejection of the body seen in "A Life" may remind us of the belief attributed to the early Gnostics that the flesh belonged to the hateful and despicable world of the senses which had been created by an evil god to estrange humanity from the unimaginably remote realm of purity governed by the good deity. A curious episode in

The Castle seems to invite such an interpretation. Waiting in the snow for the Castle official Klamm to emerge from the inn, K. is encouraged by the driver of Klamm's sledge to drink from one of the brandy bottles kept there. The exquisite promise of the brandy's aroma is not borne out by its actual taste:

> He pulled one out, unscrewed the cap, and took a sniff, he had to smile, it smelled so sweet, so caressing, as when you hear praise and fine words from someone of whom you are very fond and you are not at all sure what it is about and do not wish to know and are simply happy in the knowledge that it is the loved one speaking. "That's brandy?" K. wondered in some doubt, and tasted it out of curiosity. Yes, it was brandy, astonishingly, it burned and it warmed. The way it changed as you drank it, from something that was little more than a source of fragrance into a drink for a sledge driver.

One of Kafka's most provocative early interpreters, Erich Heller, found here a Gnostic outlook, according to which phenomena are most beautiful when most ethereal, most nearly spiritual, but become gross and commonplace when embodied in matter, or, as in this case, by making direct contact with the body.

The late Kafka, however, develops a new, complex attitude toward the body. An aphorism runs: "The martyrs do not reject the body; they elevate it on the cross. In this they agree with their opponents." That is, the broken body of the crucified martyr is not a mere vessel to be discarded, but the indispensable sign of spiritual triumph. Similarly, the Fasting Artist does not reject his body. He is not seeking to waste away and become a purely spiritual being. Rather, his body is the instrument of his art. His powers

In some of Kafka's later works, such as *The Castle*, scholars have detected a connection to some of the tenets of early Gnosticism. This fragment is from the Gospel of Judas in the Codex Tchacos, an ancient Egyptian papyrus containing early Gnostic texts from ca. 300 CE.

of endurance are recorded in its progressive emaciation. He would be nothing without it. Likewise, as Peter Brown has argued, the early hermits who retreated to the Egyptian desert were trying, not to damage or punish their bodies, but to transform their bodies by privation into a semblance of the spiritual body of the Resurrection:

> It was only the twisted will of fallen men that had crammed the body with unnecessary food, thereby generating in it the dire surplus of energy that showed itself in physical appetite, in anger, and in the sexual urge. In reducing the intake to which he had become accustomed, the ascetic slowly remade his body. He turned it into an exactly calibrated instrument. Its drastic physical changes, after years of ascetic discipline, registered with satisfying precision the essential, preliminary stages of the long return of the human person, body and soul together, to an original, natural and uncorrupted state. (Peter Brown, *The Body and Society: Men, Women and Sexual Renunciation in Early Christianity* [New York: Columbia University Press, 1988], p. 223)

Kafka's Fasting Artist, in a story he published just a few years before his death, does not reject his body; instead, his body is an instrument of his art, similar to the body of the ascetic, as exemplified by St. Jerome, pictured here in Albrecht Altdorfer's portrait from 1507.

The Fasting Artist suffers for his art far worse than Flaubert or the other dedicated artists whom Kafka admired. By prolonged privation he makes his body into the visible product of his devotion, something more intimately himself than a book would have been. The forty-day limit imposed by his impresario prevents him from achieving artistic perfection; and when he is neglected, and can starve indefinitely in a corner, nobody else appreciates his feat.

In all these cases, we are dealing with the individual body. But the body is also a common figure for larger human groups: the citizen body, the body politic. And Kafka uses the image in this way, especially in later stories, where his focus moves gradually from the isolated individual to the community. In "Investigations of a Dog" the dogs have a strong sense of community, living "in a single heap." Their highest joy consists in "warm togetherness," and they are constantly puzzled to understand why they live so far apart, obeying rules that are not of their own devising. The dogs in the story are unaware of the existence of humans. They do not know that their food is thrown to them by their owners, but believe that they produce it by watering the ground. The paradox that the food comes from above, not from below, is one they can live with, except for the scientifically minded narrator who starves himself in the hope of solving the riddle. But since the inborn limitations of his cognitive powers will prevent him from ever discovering that humans feed the dogs, the story gently implies that he would have done better to lead a normal, unreflective, doggy existence. In Kafka's last story, "Josefine, the Songstress or: The Mouse People," the talents of the singing mouse are dubious. She seems only to squeak, like all the other mice. Yet they gather to hear her, huddled together, "body pressed warmly to body"; they take care of her as though, in relation to her, they were a single individual, "much as a father looks after a child"; and her singing gives its listeners a quasi-physical experience of unity with all others:

> it is as if the limbs of each were loosened, as if each single, anxious individual were allowed for once to stretch out and relax to his heart's contents in the great warm bed of the people.

The body of the nation provides a unity into which even such an egoistic individual as Josefine can be absorbed. Her death, the narrator concludes, will be a deliverance from the special status that she mistakenly desires:

> So perhaps we shall not miss so very much after all, while Josefine, for her part, delivered from earthly afflictions, which however to her mind are the privilege of chosen spirits, will happily lose herself in the countless throng of the heroes of her people, and soon, since we pursue no history, be accorded the heightened deliverance of being forgotten along with all her brethren.

FOUR

Institutions

●

KAFKA WAS FASCINATED by institutions. Institutions are types of social organizations serving particular purposes, such as the household, the family, the business corporation, the government ministry, the school, the hospital, the prison. The word *institution* tends to slip from its general meaning to a more specific sense, denoting especially those institutions where people are confined, allegedly for their own good and often against their own wishes, such as old people's homes, mental asylums, and jails. A similar ambiguity inhabits the word Kafka used, *Anstalt*. He uses it to refer to the organization where he worked, the Arbeiter-Unfall-Versicherungs-Anstalt für das Königreich Böhmen (Workers' Accident Insurance Institute for the Kingdom of

Kafka explored not only how institutions such as the military and mental homes oppress the bodies and minds of their inmates but also what the possibilities were for resistance and escape. In this photograph taken sometime between 1918 and 1919, US soldiers stationed at Camp Hancock, in Augusta, Georgia, engage in military exercises.

Bohemia), but in different contexts it can mean an educational institution (*Erziehungsanstalt*) or lunatic asylum (*Irrenanstalt*). In the later twentieth century, sociologists paid close attention to institutions, particularly to those which exerted the greatest control over their inmates. Erving Goffman's study of mental homes, *Asylums* (1961), examines an instance of "total institutions" which try to dictate the entire behavior of their inhabitants. Michel Foucault's *Discipline and Punish* (1975) considers how institutions associated with justice, especially the prison, and with training, such as the army, shape the very bodies of those assigned to them. Kafka, however, was there before them. His work contains a deeply felt, sensitively rendered analysis of institutions, not only showing how they oppress the bodies and minds of their inmates, but also, in his later works, exploring possibilities of resistance and escape.

The Law of the Family

The first institution that anyone encounters is the family. For Kafka, the family is the place where oppression starts. The oppression Gregor Samsa suffers from his family is vividly embodied in the layout of his room, which has three doors (Gregor locks them all at night), at each of which a member of his family, his father, mother, and sister, knocks, urging him to get up and go to work. Kafka spoke of parental love as smothering, and of family life as a battleground. "I always felt my parents as persecutors," he told Felice in 1912.

> Parents only want to drag one down to them, into the old times from which one would like to ascend with a sigh of relief; they want to do this out of love, of course, but that's what's so awful.

Eight years later he described to Milena the awfulness of "sinking into this circle of kindness, of love—you don't know my letter to my father—the wriggling of flies glued to a stick." But, he added, even this had its good side: "One person fights at Marathon, another in the dining-room, the god of war and the goddess of victory are everywhere." Kafka is not here complaining about parental unkindness or abuse. For him, it is the sticky bond created by parental affection that is so hard to resist. In his two great stories of family conflict, *The Judgment* and *The Transformation*, the heroes are doomed by their love for their parents. Georg Bendemann is certainly a selfish and neglectful son, who has given no thought to how his father will fare after Georg's marriage, and his pro-testations of affection are clearly designed to stop his father's awkward questions about the friend in Russia, and, as the father rightly charges, to "cover him up." But when, obeying his father's sentence, Georg throws himself off the bridge, he reverts to a childish identity as "the outstanding gymnast who had once been his parents' pride," and his last words are: "Dear parents, I did always love you." As for Gregor Samsa, the loyal son who has supported the family single-handedly since his father's bank-ruptcy, he learns after his transformation that his parents had put some money by and did not really need his self-sacrifice; his family lose interest in him, cease to feed him, and use his room to store junk; and finally, when Gregor threatens their economic interests by frightening away their lodgers, they decide, by the illogic typical of Kafka's characters, that the insect cannot be Gregor. Their self-deception emerges from the confu-sion of pronouns when the sister first denies that "it" can be Gregor, then exclaims: "he's at it again!" The alternation between "it" and "he" dehu-manizes Gregor and turns him into a piece of animated garbage. Yet he feels no resentment:

His thoughts went back to his family with tenderness and love. His own opinion that he must disappear was if anything even firmer than his sister's.

Like Georg, he dies full of submissive love for the family who have discarded him.

Kafka repeatedly complains that adults seek to suppress children's individuality. A photograph of Kafka as a small boy shows him (to quote Walter Benjamin's description) "in a sort of greenhouse setting, wearing a tight, heavily lace-trimmed, almost embarrassing child's suit." One feels for the little boy who gazes sadly out of the frame, obviously wishing to be somewhere else, and who, as Benjamin reminds us, later wrote the fantasy "Longing to be a Red Indian." Looking back, Kafka admitted that he was rather a pampered and difficult child, but he remembered mainly being the victim of various authorities, ranging from his father to the servant who took him to school and frightened him every day by threatening to tell the teacher about his naughtiness. Kafka knew well that worse things happened to many children. *The Man Who Disappeared*, the story of an essentially innocent boy adrift in America, begins by baldly introducing "the seventeen-year-old Karl Rossmann, who had been sent to America by his unfortunate parents because a maid had seduced him and had a child by him." Not only does Karl retain his love for the parents who have so monstrously punished the victim, but it becomes clear that he has suffered abuse, having been forced by the maid into an act of intercourse which he found "disgusting," made him feel "a shocking helplessness," and left him "in tears."

In his fierce criticism of contemporary child rearing Kafka agreed with many enlightened educators. Kafka was particularly impressed by the radical psychoanalyst Otto Gross, whom he met through Max Brod in 1917; they discussed founding a journal to be called *Pages on Combating the Will to Power*. Gross took drugs, had many lovers (including Frieda Weekley, later the wife of D. H. Lawrence), and considered the conventional family the source of patriarchal authority, which needed to be overthrown by revolution. He spoke from experience: in 1913 his father, a professor of criminal law whose lectures Kafka had attended at university, had Otto committed to a psychiatric clinic, on the grounds that his belief in free love proved his insanity. He was released after a public outcry. Gross's emphasis on paternal authority no doubt helped Kafka to compose the "Letter to his Father."

Kafka took a close interest in education. He persuaded Felice to help in a home for young Jewish refugees in Berlin, and advised her in many letters on how to handle the children. In 1921 Kafka wrote several letters to his sister Elli about bringing up children. She was considering sending her ten-year-old son Felix away to school. Kafka recommended A. S. Neill's progressive school at Hellerau. He quoted to her Swift's account of how children are brought up in Lilliput, emphasizing and elucidating the view that parents were the last people to be entrusted with bringing up their children. Parental love, he explained, was a kind of selfishness.

Irish satirist Jonathan Swift (1667–1745) published *Gulliver's Travels* in 1726. This illustration of Gulliver among the Lilliputians was published in an 1865 London edition of the novel.

Parents cannot help projecting their wishes onto the child and trying to shape the child accordingly. Hence they resort to two methods of education: tyranny and slavery:

> These, born from selfishness, are the parents' two methods of education: tyranny and slavery of every shade. The expression of tyranny can be very tender ("You must believe me, because I'm your mother!") and that of slavery very proud ("You are my son, therefore I will make you into my savior!") but they are two dreadful methods, two methods of anti-education, designed to stamp the child back into the ground from which it emerged.

Children had to be removed from "the stuffy, poison-laden, child-starving air of the nicely furnished family drawing-room."

The family, for Kafka, is also the place where power, guilt, law, and punishment originate. The "Letter to his Father" describes how Hermann Kafka laid down strict laws on good behavior from which he himself was exempt. From such experiences Kafka came to imagine law as a mechanism of power, going back to family relationships. Children, dependent on their parents and trapped by the bonds of love, acquiesce in the power that rules their small lives, and internalize the standards of behavior which they later pass on to their own offspring. The acquiescence that secures the law of the family is carried over into adult life as acquiescence in social institutions. As the Marxist philosopher Louis Althusser argued, and as Kafka knew long before him, the authority of society is based for the most part not on physical coercion, but on people's acceptance of social institutions, even of those that damage them.

A LILLIPUTIAN EDUCATION

Their notions relating to the duties of parents and children differ extremely from ours. For since the conjunction of male and female is founded upon the great law of nature, in order to propagate and continue the species, the Lilliputians will needs have it, that men and women are joined together like other animals, by the motives of con-cupiscence; and that their tenderness towards their young proceeds from the like natural principle: for which reason they will never allow, that a child is under any obligation to his father for begetting him, or his mother for bringing him into the world; which, considering the miseries of human life, was neither a benefit in itself, nor intend-ed so by his parents, whose thoughts in their love-encounters were otherwise employed. Upon these, and the like reasonings, their opinion is, that parents are the last of all others to be trusted with the education of their own children: and therefore they have in every town public nurseries, where all parents, except cottagers and labourers, are obliged to send their infants of both sexes to be reared and educated when they come to the age of twenty moons, at which time they are supposed to have some rudiments of docility.

Swift, Gulliver's Travels

· · · · ·

Trials

Between the law of the family, and the mysterious law that invades the life of Josef K. in *The Trial*, comes the novel set in America, *The Man Who Disappeared*, which is structured as a series of trials in which the well-intentioned hero, Karl Rossmann, is repeatedly found guilty. We have already seen how he is banished to America for being a victim of abuse. On the ship he befriends a stoker who complains bitterly but obscurely of the injustices inflicted on him by the ship's engineer. Anxious to help, Karl accompanies the stoker to the Captain's office, and is recognized by his uncle, an emigrant who has worked his way up to become a wealthy and respected Senator. The stoker is left to have his case decided by the Captain, in ominous terms:

> "The stoker will get whatever he deserves," said the Senator, "and whatever the captain determines. [. . .] it may be a question of justice, but at the same time it's a matter of discipline."

Despite the faint protests of Karl, who still thinks that justice can be objectively determined by fair-minded people, the Senator equates justice with discipline and both with the will of the Captain, the supreme authority onboard ship.

Karl passes under the authority of his uncle. One evening a friend, Mr. Pollunder, invites Karl to visit his country house near New York and meet his daughter Klara. The uncle consents with some reluctance. After various misadventures at the country house, Karl receives a note from his uncle, containing a third-class ticket to San Francisco, and banishing him forever because of what proves to have been a fatal act of disobedience. This pattern of offense and punishment recurs throughout Kafka's work. A slight misdemeanor, barely recognizable as such or defined by an arbitrary code, meets with a punishment of utterly disproportionate severity. The prisoner in the story *In the Penal Colony* is a soldier whose duty it had been to mount guard outside his officer's door, and to rise and salute the door every hour, but who fell asleep and when struck across the face with a whip was bold enough to offer resistance. For this crime he is sentenced to death by torture. The Country Doctor, left on the point of freezing to death in a wintry landscape, laments: "If you once respond to a faulty ring on the night-bell—it can never be made good." The model case of this conception of punishment is set out in "The Knock at the Manor Gate" (see sidebar).

$$\cdot \ \cdot \ \cdot \ \cdot \ \cdot$$

THE KNOCK AT THE MANOR GATE

It was summer, a hot day. With my sister I was passing the gate of a great house on our way home. I cannot tell now whether she knocked on the gate out of mischief or out of absence of mind, or merely threatened it with her fist and did not knock at all. A hundred paces further along the road, which here turned to the left, the village began. We did not know it, but no sooner had we passed the first house than people appeared and made friendly or warning signs to us; some were even terrified, bowed down by terror. They pointed toward the manor house that we had passed and reminded us of the knock on the gate. The owner of the manor, they said, would charge us with it, the interrogation would begin immediately. I was very calm and also tried to calm my sister. Probably she had not struck the door at all, and if she had it could never be proved. I tried to make this clear to the people round us; they listened to me, but refrained from passing any opinion. Later they said that not only my sister but I too, as her brother, would be charged. I nodded and smiled. We all gazed back at the manor, as one watches a distant cloud of smoke and waits for the flames to appear. And right enough, we presently saw horsemen riding in through the wide-open gate. Dust rose, concealing everything; only the points of the tall spears glittered. And hardly had the troop vanished into the manor courtyard than they seemed to have turned their horses again and were on their way to us. I urged my sister to leave, saying I myself would set everything right. She refused to leave me. I told her she should at least change so as to appear in better clothes before these gentlemen. At last she obeyed and set out on the long road to our home. Already the horsemen were beside us, and even before dismounting they enquired after my sister. She wasn't here at the moment, came the apprehensive reply, but she would come later. The answer was received with indifference; the important thing seemed their having found me. The chief members of the party appeared to be a young lively fellow, who was a judge, and his silent assistant, who was called Assmann. I was commanded to enter the village inn. Slowly, shaking my head, tugging at my braces, I set off, watched keenly by the gentlemen. I still half-believed that a word would be enough to free me, a city man, and with honor too, from these peasants. But as soon as I had stepped over the threshold of the parlor, the judge, who had hastened in front and was already awaiting me, said: "I'm sorry for this man." And it was beyond all possibility of doubt that by this he did not mean my present state, but something that was going to happen to me. The room looked more like a prison cell than an inn parlor. Great flagstones, dark, quite bare walls, into one of which an iron ring was fixed, in the middle something that was half a pallet, half an operating table.

Could I now endure any other air than prison air? That is the great question, or rather it would be if I still had any prospect of release.

· · · · ·

Karl's next escapade in *The Man Who Disappeared* illustrates how a trial, rather than identifying the culprit, can put a predetermined victim inescapably in the wrong. Working as a lift-boy at the Hotel Occidental, he meets an old acquaintance, the tramp Robinson, who is hopelessly drunk. To get Robinson to bed, Karl needs to leave his post by the lift. For doing so, he is arraigned by the Head Waiter. Malicious allegations that he spends his nights in debauchery seem confirmed by the discovery of Robinson. All Karl's explanations are turned against him, so that even his supporters believe him to be deceitful, and he is again expelled. Being put on trial is itself proof that one must be guilty.

The same law seems to operate in *The Trial*, but in a subtler way. Although the novel was inspired partly by the "trial" (*Gerichtshof*) to which Kafka was subjected by Felice and her supporters when their engagement was dissolved, it contains no actual court proceedings. After his arrest, Josef K. is summoned before the Examining Magistrate, to whom, instead of waiting to be questioned, he blusters about his innocence. Thereafter the Court leaves him alone until the scene where, waiting in the Cathedral for a business contact, K. finds himself summoned from a small pulpit by a clergyman who proves to be the Prison Chaplain, and who warns him that he is thought to be guilty. The Court's only further move is to send K. his executioners.

These fantastic events can be related to the actual legal system with which Kafka was familiar. Two conceptions of law were in conflict among jurists in Kafka's day. One was the strictly Kantian philosophy of law enshrined in the legal code of the German Empire (1871). Assuming that the criminal was morally responsible for his actions, this code focused only on the act committed, prescribing punishment in accordance with the nature of the crime (though with allowance for mitigating circumstances).

This manuscript, handwritten in the original German, is the beginning of the final chapter of Kafka's *The Trial* (*Der Prozess*), published posthumously in 1925.

The Austrian legal code, by contrast, defined crime not only as an act but also with reference to the "evil intent" of the defendant, thus making the defendant's motivation crucial to the determination of guilt. Accordingly it became an axiom of Austrian law that there could be guilt without illegality: somebody might plan a crime but be prevented from carrying it out by an external accident. In Kafka's novel, Josef K. never asks, and nobody troubles to tell him, what, if anything, he is charged with. The warders who arrest him assert that the Court is attracted to guilt, and therefore he must be guilty in order to have been arrested:

> Our authorities, as far as I know them, and I know only the lowest grades, do not go in search of guilt in the population but are, as it says in the law, drawn to guilt and must send us warders out.

Although it is made clear that K.'s lawsuit is "not a trial before the ordinary court," the law of his trial takes to a caricatural extreme the tendency of the Austrian legal system to concentrate on the criminal rather than the crime. The authorities are interested not in the act Josef K. may have committed but in his guilt (*Schuld*), and the word's meaning slides from "responsibility for an act" to "subjective feelings of guilt." Being accused seems to mean being a special type of person, destined for humiliation, and ultimately execution.

Accordingly, the narrative of *The Trial* concerns, not so much the Court's dealings with K., but rather K.'s response to his arrest. Despite his protests, he does what the warders tell him, thus accepting in practice the authority of the unknown Court even as he protests against it. He accepts it partly because it is an institution, and he knows automatically how to respond to institutional authority. To explain such acceptance, Althusser gives the example of hearing a call "Hey, you there!" and turning round, accepting that you are the subject of the summons even though it was not addressed to you by name. Thus the individual lets himself be "interpellated" (Althusser's word)—placed within a social and ideological system. Josef K. similarly lets himself be interpellated by the Court, long before he is summoned as an individual by the Chaplain's call "Josef K.!"

The Court also exploits K.'s insecurity. Indeed, the novel could be read as a series of maneuvers in which the Court, while hypocritically professing not to interfere in K.'s life, engenders in him a feeling of guilt which eventually so dominates him that he submits to his executioners. On the other hand, his protestations of innocence, without seeking to learn what he is charged with, might suggest an inner awareness of guilt which the Court has awakened and which K. is trying, with ever-increasing difficulty, to repress. To the Chaplain, K. protests that he is not guilty, and nobody can be:

Kafka's *The Trial* has been adapted for the screen several times. British playwright Harold Pinter adapted the novel for the 1993 film, in which Kyle MacLachlan plays Joseph K. and Anthony Hopkins plays the Chaplain.

"But I am not guilty," K. said. "It's a mistake. How can a human being ever be guilty? We are all human beings here after all, each the same as the other." "That is right," said the priest, "but everyone who is guilty always talks like that."

By this point the word *Schuld* seems to have slid in a new direction: from legal culpability and subjective feelings of guilt it has moved to being in the wrong, not in a legal but rather in a moral, conceivably even in a theological, sense. K. reasons that human beings are weak and fallible; therefore, all human beings incur guilt, and it makes no sense to single out one for arrest and punishment. The Chaplain gives the uncompromising answer that just such claims are made by the guilty to exculpate themselves, implying that guilt may be universal and still deserve punishment. Earlier in the novel, K. has seen an image of justice as a woman in rapid motion, with wings on her feet, looking more like the goddess of victory and the hunt. The Court inexorably hunts its victims down, like the hunting dogs in an aphorism dating from 1917:

> The hunting dogs are still playing in the courtyard, but the game will not escape them, no matter how fast it may already be flying through the woods.

The strongest suggestion that the Court is not simply an exploitative authority, but also the agent of some higher power, comes in the parable told to Josef K. by the Chaplain, in which a man denied entrance to the Law by the doorkeeper sees, as he dies, the radiance shining from the Law, and asks a question he should have asked long before:

> "Everybody strives for the law," says the man. "How is it that in all these years nobody except myself has asked for admittance?" The doorkeeper realizes that the man has reached the end of his life and, to penetrate his imperfect hearing, he roars at him: "Nobody else could gain admittance here, this entrance was meant only for you. I shall now go and close it."

Perhaps Josef K.'s arrest was not only an affliction but also, had he known it, an opportunity. To gain some inkling of what that opportunity was, and of why Josef K. reacts to his arrest and trial only negatively, we need to consider what kind of person he is.

The Organization Man

Josef K., like other Kafka protagonists, embodies the type required and produced by modern institutions of work, commerce, and government. To see how work is represented in Kafka, we may turn back to *The Transformation* and to Gregor Samsa's reflections on his job as a commercial traveler:

> "O God," he thought, "what an exhausting job I've chosen! On the move day in, day out. The business worries are far worse than they are on the actual premises at home, and on top of that I'm saddled with the strain of all this traveling, the anxiety about train connections, the bad and irregular meals, the constant stream of changing faces with no chance of any warmer, lasting companionship. The devil take it all!"

Not only is his job—displaying samples of cloth to potential customers—tiring and unsatisfying, but Gregor is closely monitored by his employers. In the office, the boss sits on his desk, addresses the staff from on high, and makes them come close up to him because he is hard of hearing. Gregor fears that if he reports sick his boss will come along in person, accompanied by the doctor, who will never accept that a patient is ill instead of malingering. In fact his failure to appear at the station leads to a personal visit from the chief clerk, who becomes more and more intimidating, first hinting that Gregor may be misappropriating cash, and then warning him: "your position in

Kafka in 1923 or 1924.

the firm is by no means assured [. . .] for some time past your work has been most unsatisfactory."

Modern work, as represented here, is abstract and hierarchical. Gregor has no relation to manual labor or primary production. Showing samples and collecting payments, he is a mere middleman in the commercial process. His firm displays its hierarchy by the exaggerated elevation of the boss on his desk, the close monitoring to which it apparently subjects its employees, and the monstrous threats that follow the slightest misdemeanor.

The world of abstraction and hierarchy requires a particular type of person to operate in it. Gregor is an unhappy and inadequate version of a type of which aspects are embodied in several Kafka protagonists. From Gregor, Georg Bendemann, Josef K., K. in *The Castle*, and the Country Doctor, we can distill an ideal type of the modern professional man. He is orderly and calculating, as his job demands. Gregor's work is ruled by train timetables. Having missed both the 5:00 a.m. and the 7:00 a.m. train, he resolves to catch the train at 8:00; on waking he sees that the time is 6:30; his mother knocks on his door at 6:45; he decides to get out of bed by 7:15, but is alarmed by the arrival of the chief clerk at 7:10. Josef K. gets his breakfast in bed every day at 8:00, works in his office until 9:00 p.m., and then socializes with influential officials until 11:00. Even his sexual life is fitted into his routine: he goes once a week to a girl called Elsa who "received her visitors only in bed."

Georg Bendemann is at ease with numbers: he reflects that the turnover of his business has increased fivefold, and deplores the low commercial figures cited by his friend in Russia. K. in *The Castle* is a land surveyor, dedicated to mathematical abstraction.

The professional man generally works for an organization that is hierarchically structured. While Gregor has a lowly position in his firm, bullied by the chief clerk, Josef K. *is* a chief clerk, as he proudly informs the Examining Magistrate. His arrogance is evident from his treatment of the three junior employees who are assigned to accompany him to the bank after his arrest. They are so inferior that he does not consider them colleagues; all irritate him, especially the one whose facial rictus freezes his features in an involuntary grin "which common humanity unfortunately forbade one to joke about"; and during the day K. wastes their time by summoning them repeatedly to his office for no reason other than to observe their demeanor. Toward his superiors, however, he is obsequious. He jockeys for power with his nearest rival, the deputy director. The officials with whom he spends his evenings are judges and lawyers, along with some junior colleagues who serve only to amuse the company. The Country Doctor is not a private practitioner but "employed by the district" as a "medical officer" (*Amtsarzt*). K. seeks to enter the organization of the Castle which has apparently summoned him by mistake, and wishes to bypass the ranks of secretaries by making direct contact with one of the highest officials.

The authority of men in these hierarchies is best embodied in an upright military carriage, a massive physique, and a fierce look. Even Gregor Samsa has done military service, as a photograph of him in uniform shows, and K. recalls his military service as "those happy times." Bendemann senior has a war wound, and still strikes his son as a "giant" even before he leaps upright. When Samsa senior appears restored to vitality, he is upright, with bushy eyebrows, and wearing a uniform. Gregor is "astonished at the gigantic size of the soles of his boots," which seem able to crush the cowering insect. Imposing stature is shared by K.'s influential friend Staatsanwalt Hasterer, a "gigantic man who could have hidden him [K.] in his overcoat." Hasterer is a lawyer with rare skill in intimidating his opponents: "many people drew back in fright before his outstretched forefinger." We never meet any of the judges in the Court, but K. sees a picture of one in the Advocate's kitchen:

> It showed a man in the robes of a judge. He was sitting on a high throne-like chair whose gilding stood out prominently in the picture. The unusual thing about it was that this judge was not sitting in tranquil dignity but was pressing his left arm hard against the back and side of the chair and had his right arm completely free and just held the other arm of the chair with this hand as if his intention was to spring up at the next moment with a violent and perhaps outraged gesture to utter something decisive or even pronounce judgment. The defendant had to be imagined at the foot of the steps, whose upper ones, covered in yellow carpet, were visible in the picture.

Yet K. is also assured that the judge is in reality a tiny man who sits not on a throne but on a kitchen chair covered by a horse blanket. His intimidating appearance results from artistic convention. There is a hint here that authority results from the performance of authority and from the resultant acquiescence of the victim. In the parable of the doorkeeper, the doorkeeper likewise intimidates the man from the country by his bulk, his fur coat, his huge nose, and his big beard.

But suppose the man from the country had challenged him? Suppose K. had challenged the Court instead of acquiescing in its authority by giving all his time to his case?

These possibilities remain hypothetical, because, as Kafka shows, success within an institution requires one to accept its rules, including its system of hierarchy, so that anything different becomes intolerable, even unthinkable. Josef K. is the supreme example of a professional man committed to order. His arrest strikes him principally as the cause of disorder which must be tidied up: "But once this order was restored, then every trace of those events would be eliminated and everything would resume its old course." Nevertheless, he becomes obsessed with the Court, picturing it in the image of his own organization, with a vast opaque hierarchy of officials, and deciding to deal with it by submitting a lengthy document. If, however, the Court represents something missing from K.'s life, perhaps a moral dimension that has been lacking, then that is something he cannot perceive. The Court Painter describes to him the three possible outcomes of a trial: complete acquittal, which is recorded only in legends; apparent acquittal, which may be followed immediately by re-arrest; and prolongation, which means dragging out the proceedings so that one is never condemned but also never free of one's lawsuit. K. rejects the first because it has no place in his mind-set, declaring brusquely: "Mere legends don't alter my opinion." He is trapped less by the Court than by the limitations of his consciousness, the situation drastically portrayed in an aphorism: "The bony structure of his own forehead blocks his way; he batters himself bloody against his own forehead." Or he may be compared to the Country Doctor who is so locked into his routine that even after the unearthly horses have emerged from the pigsty to carry him instantaneously to his patient, he cannot at first perceive the huge wound until alerted to it by the horses' neighing.

Habituation to routine prevents Kafka's characters from perceiving realities that are at odds with their institutional mentalities. But his narratives repeatedly show how these incongruous realities, breaking in from outside, assail, weaken, and finally destroy the uncomprehending protagonists. Georg Bendemann is reduced to a helpless child by his reinvigorated father; the Country Doctor ends up naked in the snow; while Josef K.'s breakdown is a psychologically subtle and long-drawn-out process, involving denial of his problem, a pathetic search for human solidarity (from his landlady, Fräulein Bürstner, and the Chaplain), and also a predatory sexuality that emerges as soon as the armor plating of his professional routine is pierced. His search for human support is most apparent when he tells the Chaplain that unlike most Court officials, he feels he can trust him and speak openly to him. The legend of the doorkeeper with which the Chaplain responds is among other things a veiled warning not to make oneself dependent on other people—as the man from the country does with the doorkeeper—but to make one's own decisions. Similarly, as the Advocate tells K., the Court seeks to eliminate defense lawyers: "the accused man must be left to his own devices."

In thus evoking the strength and vulnerability of the modern professional man, Kafka comes close to the analysis of this type put forward by his contemporary, the sociologist Max Weber. Weber undertook to explain the emergence of the "spirit of capitalism," which involves cautious, rational, long-term planning, in contrast to hasty accumulation or rash speculation. He found an "elective affinity" between this mind-set and the conduct instilled by early Protestantism, which eliminated all magical means of salvation and adjured the believer to work hard in his calling in the hope that worldly success would prove God's favor.

· · · · ·

WEBER'S PROFESSIONAL MAN

German sociologist and economist Max Weber's (1864–1920) *Economy and Society* was published posthumously in 1925.

This innerworldly asceticism had a number of distinctive consequences not found in any other religion. This religion demanded of the believer not celibacy, as in the case of the monk, but the avoidance of all erotic pleasure; not poverty, but the elimination of all idle and exploitative enjoyment of unearned wealth and income, and the avoidance of all feudalistic, sensuous ostentation of wealth; not the ascetic death-in-life of the cloister, but an alert, rationally controlled patterning of life, and the avoidance of all surrender to the beauty of the world, to art, or to one's own moods and emotions. The clear and uniform goal of this asceticism was the disciplining and methodical organization of conduct. Its typical representative was the "man of a vocation" or "professional" (*Berufsmensch*), and its unique result was the rational organization of social relationships.

Max Weber, Economy and Society: An Outline of Interpretive Sociology, *ed. Guenther Roth and Claus Wittich (New York: Bedminster, 1968), p. 556*

· · · · ·

Weber worried, however, that this model of the self was being transformed into the "bureaucratic man" dependent on an order provided from outside, and unable to take decisions as an autonomous and principled person. That applies to Josef K. Entirely devoted to his work, detached from his family (he fails to visit his mother and neglects the niece who is attending school in the city), without cultural enjoyments, even his sexuality confined to a hygienic weekly session, he is unprepared for anything unfamiliar and unable to respond to it without resorting to the behavior that has brought him professional success in his institution.

Weber is the theorist of bureaucracy, whereas Kafka is its satirist. Bureaucracy, according to Weber, requires a hierarchical organization in which each official has clearly delimited tasks and responsibilities. These are to be carried out in accordance with stipulated rules and in an impersonal manner, irrespective of the private character of the official (so corruption and nepotism must be excluded), and recorded on paper. The conduct of business by rules means that bureaucratic work must be rendered calculable and predictable. Rough and recalcitrant reality must be replaced by an abstract counterpart. This bureaucratic ideal is satirized in *The Castle*, in which a vast and supposedly flawless organization has the effect of insulating the officials from real life. If one telephones the Castle, only an unlikely chance can get one through to an actual official, who in any case will merely pick up the receiver for a joke; the buzzing noise one hears is that of constant telephoning going on *within* the Castle, confirming its isolation from the outside world. Permanently exhausted, the bureaucrats sleep in their offices and amuse themselves by seducing village girls. What they cannot deal with is the concrete reality of an individual client. Hence every effort is made to prevent a client from actually making contact with the official competent to deal with his case, as Klamm's secretary Bürgel explains to K.:

> "And now, sir, consider the possibility of a party, as a result of certain circumstances, any circumstances, and despite the obstacles that have been described to you and that usually prove quite adequate, nevertheless, in the middle of the night, surprising a secretary who possesses a certain competence regarding the case concerned. Presumably such a possibility never occurred to you before, am I right? I quite believe it. Nor need it have done, since it almost never happens. What an oddly and very specifically shaped, agile little granule such a party would need to be to pass through the supreme sieve. You think it can't happen at all? You're right, it can't. But one night—who can vouch for everything?—it does happen."

When the impossible occurs, and an inquiring client coincides with a competent official, then, Bürgel continues, the official is actually helpless with delight and bound to grant the client everything he asks. But even that does not undermine the bureaucratic organization. For the client to whom Bürgel is explaining this, K., has fallen asleep with the effort of reaching Bürgel's room (albeit he stumbled into it by accident), and does not realize that he has met an official who can actually do something for him. When K. wakens, Bürgel continues his monologue: "Of course some opportunities are too big to be taken advantage of, as it were; there are things that fail for no reason other than themselves." Bureaucracy here is not only an object of satire but a metaphor for something greater: for contact with whatever lies beyond the bounds of human life.

In his portrayal of bureaucracy, Kafka captures another characteristic of modern institutions: the invisibility of their rulers. Premodern institutions established their authority by ceremonial. "All things in life," wrote J. H. Huizinga about the Middle Ages, "were of a proud or cruel publicity." Even punishment was a solemn public ceremony, in which a murderer passed through crowds, mounted the scaffold, and was exhorted to repent for the edification of the spectators. In Kafka's fiction, organizations are headed by managers and directors. Traditional rulers appear only as ineffectual figureheads, like the Emperor in "A Leaf from an Old Manuscript" who, unable to drive away the nomads who have invaded his city, watches

The authority of premodern institutions and even the punishments they meted out were established by ceremony. This image shows the public execution on February 28, 1616, at the Rossmarkt (horse market) in Frankfurt of ringleader Vincent Fettmilch and his co-conspirators after the Fettmilch Riot.

them from the window of his palace. In *The Castle* the traditional rule of Count Westwest exists in name only. The Count's flag flies from the battlements, but he never appears, and the bureaucrats, especially Klamm, enjoy the superstitious respect formerly reserved for royalty.

Punishment has likewise retreated to private spaces. In the most horrific episode of *The Trial*, the warders who arrested K., and of whose conduct K. complained to the Examining Magistrate, appear in a lumber room in K.'s bank, being whipped for their misdemeanors by a man in a leather outfit. The hint of homosexual sadism here confirms that the punishment is a vicarious realization of K.'s unconscious desires. Consciously, K. is shocked by the obvious and extreme cruelty of the punishment, tries ineffectually to buy the Whipper off, and at last slams the door on the victim, whose scream "did not seem to come from a man but from a tortured instrument." This revelation of the violence underpinning the Court's authority anticipates the final chapter, where K. is taken by his executioners to a remote quarry and has a knife twisted in his heart.

Kafka knew that in the civilized modern world violence was banished to concealed rooms in police stations and prisons, and to colonial settings far from Europe. For somebody who never left Europe, he gives an astonishingly perceptive portrayal of colonialism and violence in the story *In the Penal Colony*, written about the same time as the Whipper scene of *The Trial*; it bears comparison with *Heart of Darkness*, which is based on Conrad's first-hand knowledge of colonial exploitation in the Belgian Congo. One of Kafka's uncles, Joseph Loewy, worked from 1891 to 1902 in the Congo as administrator on a railway which was built by forced labor; his experiences seem to have inspired a fragment in Kafka's notebook about "building the railway in the interior of the Congo," and to have shaped *In the Penal Colony* by coalescing with reports of Captain

The Dreyfus Affair was a controversy that erupted in France in the 1890s and 1900s over the conviction of treason and subsequent sentencing to solitary confinement at the penal colony on Devil's Island of Jewish artillery officer Captain Alfred Dreyfus. This photograph shows the courtroom during Dreyfus's espionage trial in Rennes, France, with Dreyfus standing at center.

Dreyfus's unjust imprisonment in the French penal settlement of Devil's Island. Kafka would also have known from the press about the genocidal suppression by the German colonial authorities of the Herero uprising in Southwest Africa (now Namibia). In the story, set in a French-speaking colony, an officer shows a European visitor an "apparatus" (a word used not only for machinery but for the apparatus of administration) designed for punishment. A prisoner inserted into it has his crime inscribed on his skin by needles during a twelve-hour period which ends with his death. The prisoner is not otherwise told his sentence: he learns it "on his body" (*an seinem Leibe*), a phrase which, as Paul Peters has discovered, also features in German discussions of how to treat the surviving Hereros: they were to feel the consequences of their rebellion "on their body" (*am eigenen Leibe*). The prisoner has been struck across the face with a horsewhip for a small infraction of duty; in 1894 the Socialist leader August Bebel shocked the German Reichstag by displaying the hippopotamus-hide whips that were used, despite official denials, in the German colonies. Another aspect of the colonial mentality appears in the officer's insistence on wearing a heavy uniform, which represents the homeland; similarly, British administrators in nineteenth-century India insisted on retaining symbolic contact with their homeland by wearing stuffy European clothes in 104-degree heat and even donning an evening suit every night for dinner.

Oppression in Kafka's penal colony may change its character, but looks unlikely to vanish. In the past, punishments were a public spectacle. They are now conducted shamefacedly in a remote valley. Although the Old Commandant, to whose authoritarian legacy the officer is devoted, is dead, his successor lacks the courage to abolish inhumane punishments and is preoccupied by technical progress (building extensions to the harbor). The only sign of hope lies with the traveler from whose perspective the story is told. Urged by the officer to support traditional punishments, the traveler considers various excuses (he is a foreigner who should mind his own business; cultural relativism would suggest that European standards should not be expected in the tropics, and so on), but at last pulls himself together and says firmly: "No." A courageous liberal conscience can just conceivably make a difference.

The morbid cruelty of the punishment machine in this story prompts the question, unavoidable in any discussion of Kafka, whether his works in some sense prophesy the Third Reich and the atrocities of the mid-twentieth century. To simplistic versions of this question the answer is obviously negative. Kafka could not see into the future. But his insight into the mechanisms of power, authority, and violence makes one reluctant to dismiss the question entirely. Part at least of the answer is that Kafka, as the preceding paragraphs have shown, was exceptionally perceptive about the working of institutions in his own day. He shows how easy it is, if you work in an institution, to lose sight of any values beyond those promoted by the institution for its specific purposes. This attitude is illustrated not only by Josef K. but by the Whipper, who says: "I am appointed to whip, so I whip." The concentration camp workers who later asserted that they were only doing their job were not saying anything new; they were simply following out the logic of institutions which Kafka had already explored.

Moreover, the structure of institutions, as Erving Goffman has shown, is similar whether their purposes are apparently benign or malign. Prisons, monasteries, asylums, and camps are all total institutions. On entering a total institution, the inmate is subjected to various forms of what Goffman calls "mortification." One is physically separated from the outside world and from the role one played there and from whatever respect accompanied it. One loses some or all of one's possessions, and must wear institutional clothing; one is known either by a new name or by an unduly familiar version of one's own. One must treat staff with deference signalized not only in words but in one's bodily posture, undergo gratuitous humiliations, and submit to have the history of one's life, especially shameful episodes, generally known. One has little or no recourse against maltreatment by those with power over one. Much of this happens to Josef K. when he is arrested. A warder invades his bedroom; he is ordered about, mocked, and shouted at; his physical space is violated when the warders bump against him; his underclothes are confiscated, and he is told he must wear a much shabbier nightgown in the future; he is ordered to put on a black coat to meet the Inspector; and he is watched by his neighbors from across the street. Even someone less proud of his civil status would be discomposed by this treatment. The long-term effects of a trial are shown by the defendants K. meets waiting in Court offices one Sunday: though clearly from the middle and upper classes, they are poorly dressed, and when they rise to salute a Court usher, they stand with bowed backs and bent knees like beggars in the street. We may suppose that even without physical maltreatment, the moral pressure of being on trial has worn them down. Kafka's grasp of institutions, the template for which was his family, enables him to disclose patterns of oppression and subservience, ultimately underpinned by violence, that are present in some measure in all institutions, the more so as the institutions approach totality. There is an immense difference between the purposes of institutions that genuinely seek to help people, like hospitals, and those that seek to destroy them, like concentration camps and death camps, and in between there are many institutions that seek to train people (schools, the army) or simply to keep them out of society's way, but what Kafka shows us is that there is no difference in structure. Indeed, the true nature of an institution entered voluntarily, such as K.'s office, is revealingly mirrored in the hierarchical structure of an oppressive institution such as the Court.

This sounds deeply pessimistic. It seems that power and its ill effects are omnipresent. "One person fights at Marathon, another in the dining-room, the god of war and the goddess of victory are everywhere." But

Kafka's vision is not unrelievedly bleak. One of the most depressing aspects of institutions is that they gain their power from the acquiescence of their inmates. Just as the child, dependent on love and nurture from its parents, accepts their control unquestioningly and internalizes their standards, so adults inwardly acquiesce even in institutions that harm them. But that fact, which might seem to render them invulnerable, contains a germ of hope. For if one withdraws one's acquiescence, one can in theory deprive the institution of its power—in theory at least; it is much more difficult in practice. Kafka's aphorism about Atlas, the giant who in Greek mythology bore the world on his shoulders, runs: "Atlas was able to hold the opinion that, if he wanted, he could put the earth down and slip away; but he was permitted only to hold this opinion." That is, Atlas's belief in freedom existed only in his head and could never have any effect on his life. Yet even in early works by Kafka, authority looks vulnerable. After passing sentence on Georg, Bendemann senior crashes onto his bed, as though his new strength has vanished once he has used it against his son. In the parable of the doorkeeper, the doorkeeper's power consists only in his statement "I am powerful," in his

Kafka saw vulnerabilities in the authority of institutions, though his view of power could be pessimistic, as in his comment that Atlas could only believe in freedom not experience it himself. Atlas was condemned by Zeus to hold up the world after the Titans were defeated by the Olympians in the Titanomachy, or War of the Titans. This illustration of Atlas is from William Cuningham's *The Cosmographical Glasse* (1559).

intimidating appearance, and in his unverifiable claim that further in there are more doorkeepers. By acquiescing in such ill-founded authority, the man from the country wastes his life and forfeits his chance of access to the Law. Moreover, if we read the text closely (always advisable in the work of a trained lawyer), we find that the doorkeeper issues a self-contradictory command: "If you are so tempted, just try to enter in spite of my prohibition." That amounts to saying "Disobey me," and hence to a double bind in which the man from the country is trapped. An aphorism of 1917–18 formulates another double bind:

> They were given the choice of being kings or king's couriers. Like children, they all wanted to be couriers. So now there are only couriers; they dash through the world, and as there are no kings, shout their meaningless messages to one another. They would gladly put an end to their wretched lives, but they dare not because of their oath of loyalty.

There is no authority; it is by a human decision that there is no authority; yet people persist in living as if they were under authority, even though their lives are miserable and meaningless.

Some hope of evading this double bind of power is offered in *The Castle*. Coming from outside the closed society of the novel, K. is not part of the system of authority that keeps the village subservient to the Castle and its officials. The villagers regard him with suspicion, and the petty authorities, such as the schoolteachers and the landlady, scorn him for his ignorance of local laws and customs. K.'s greatest infringement of local tradition is his desire to speak directly with Klamm. For the villagers, especially the women who have had brief sexual liaisons with Klamm, such a high official cannot be approached; his name may not even be uttered. K., however, induces them to admit that a meeting with Klamm, however unprecedented, is at least possible. Thus K., the outsider, challenges and defies the traditional order of the Castle. The trouble is that by challenging the Castle he is inserting himself into its own structures of authority. The point would not be to challenge it, but to ignore it. And so for much of *The Castle* K. is torn between two impulses: to defy the Castle by breaking through its bureaucratic barriers and actually speaking to a high official; and to ignore the Castle by turning his back on it and setting up house with the village girl Frieda. His antagonism to the Castle is also an obsession with the Castle, and in pursuit of this obsession he deserts Frieda and spends many hours with the family of Barnabas, the messenger through whom he hopes to reach his goal, listening to "Castle anecdotes." Many of these concern one of the most controversial episodes of the novel. One of Barnabas's sisters, Amalia, received a coarsely worded letter from a Castle official, Sortini, summoning her to his bed. Unlike most village girls, who think such patriarchal condescension an honor, she refused. Ever since then her family have been ostracized by the villagers and have believed themselves to be in disfavor with the Castle. They have spent many hours waiting by the roadside in the hope that an official would pass to whom they could plead for mercy. Amalia's sister Olga spends her nights in the stables with Castle servants as their sexual plaything, hoping that one of them may utter something remotely helpful to the family's struggle for rehabilitation. Amalia, meanwhile, has become cold and withdrawn, devoted to tending her parents, who have been rendered prematurely decrepit by their grief at the family's disgrace. Yet, with all this, there is no sign that the Castle has done anything to harm the family, or has shown disapproval of Amalia's defiance in any concrete way. The family are the victims of their own belief in the authority of the Castle. And this belief shows its destructive effects both in Olga's self-prostitution and in Amalia's emotional withdrawal. Amalia's resistance to Sortini's predation may well be an act of dignified self-assertion; but it is futile so long as her resistance to authority holds her trapped within the structures of authority. "He who fights against dragons becomes a dragon himself," says Nietzsche's Zarathustra.

Freedom?

How does one escape from structures of authority? Various Kafka figures find a provisional and ambiguous freedom. Gregor's confinement to his room in insect form does, ironically, free him from economic and social pressures. Dr. Bucephalus sidesteps history by reading law books quietly in his study. The ape in "A Report to an Academy," faced with captivity, abandons any aspiration to "that grandiose feeling of freedom in all directions" and settles for a "way out" as a music-hall performer. In Chapter 8 of *The Castle*, K., having asserted himself by preventing Klamm from entering the sledge, finds himself alone in the snow-covered courtyard in a freedom which is empty and meaningless: "there was nothing more futile, nothing more desperate than this freedom, this waiting, this invulnerability."

When Kafka envisages true freedom from authority, he thinks not of opposing authority head on, as K. does here, but of quietly stepping aside from it. A model of such freedom appears in his diaries as early as 1911 in the form of some notes on minor literatures, inspired by his knowledge of contemporary Yiddish and Czech literature. A minor literature, in contrast to a major literature like German, is not dominated by the authority of any single great writer (like Goethe in German), so that there is scope for lively discussion and wide participation in literary life. Such a literature is sustained by national feeling. It is a "diary of a nation," a reservoir of national memory. It is politicized, while retaining enough internal autonomy to be undamaged by politics. It has room for minor talents writing about minor topics. These notes have attracted much attention in recent years, because, using examples from the Habsburg Empire riven by nationalist conflicts, they prefigure the colonial and postcolonial situation where new literatures seek to establish themselves without being intimidated by the cultural authority of the metropolis, while using a version of the metropolitan language (like Indian or African writers, for example, writing in distinctive forms of English). Kafka is imagining a community in which a preoccupation with literature would not be a mark of eccentricity, as his seemed to his family, but rather diffused throughout the population, and in which the authority of great writers would not impede the further development of literature, as Goethe, in Kafka's opinion, blocked the path of German literature.

The notes on minor literatures imply a democratic community. How far did Kafka think in concrete political terms? As a schoolboy he sympathized with Socialism, wore a red carnation in his

Kafka believed that the authority of the great German writer Johann Wolfgang von Goethe (1749–1832), shown here in a monument in Frankfurt am Main, Germany, from 1844, blocked the path of German literature.

BATTLE OF BELMONT NOV. 23ª 1899. BOER-BRITISH WAR.

Kafka supported the Boers against the British in the Boer War (1899–1902), though the Boers were eventually defeated. This print of the Battle of Belmont is by the Chicago firm of Kurz and Allison, specialists in the production of commemorative prints of historical scenes. The town of Belmont was in the Orange Free State (later part of South Africa), an independent Boer state.

buttonhole, and supported the Boers in their war with the British (an unequal conflict which struck contemporaries as a singular example of imperialist bullying). Around 1910 he read the newspaper *Čas* (*Time*) which expressed the views of Thomas Masaryk (later the first president of the Czechoslovak Republic), and attended meetings of Masaryk's Realist Party and other Czech political groupings. The story that he attended anarchist meetings, however, seems to be a canard, based on confusion of identity with someone else called Kafka.

Kafka's social conscience is well documented. Brod reports his remarks after seeing workers injured by unsafe machinery: "How modest these people are! Instead of storming the Institute and smashing everything to pieces, they come and make requests." For some years he was reluctantly involved in an asbestos factory started by his brother-in-law, and comments in his diary about how the female employees were dehumanized by their mechanical work (see sidebar on psge 118).

In *The Man Who Disappeared* America is shown using the latest technology to subject people to a rigid mechanized order, in which the body is disciplined to the utmost efficiency and even the human solidarity implied in exchanging greetings has been abolished. A demonstration by striking metalworkers holds up Karl's journey to Pollunder's country house; we hear of building workers going on strike; and Karl increasingly sinks into an underclass of tramps and prostitutes. However, the political grouping that Kafka had most contact with was Zionism, not as an attempt to colonize territory in the Near East (early Zionists were naively optimistic about how the Arabs would welcome their settlements), but as a project for removing Jews from an increasingly anti-Semitic Europe and establishing communities based on equality, simplicity, and manual labor. He talked of emigrating to Palestine with Dora Diamant and working as a bookbinder, or else as waiter in a restaurant where she would be the cook. Rather than the practical details of Zionism, however, Kafka associated it with new forms of community such as he imagined in his later fiction, above all in "Josefine the Songstress," which takes an ironic view of the social role of the artist. Josefine, the singing mouse, believes intensely in her art and thinks it should earn her social privileges. To the other mice, her art is negligible, for instead of singing she only squeaks, like other mice. Yet they flock to her performances, not because her squeaking or piping has artistic merit, but because it enhances their solidarity by symbolizing their national identity:

KAFKA ON FACTORY WORKERS

Yesterday in the factory. The girls in their unbearably dirty and loosened clothes, with their hair as untidy as when they woke up, with the expression on their faces frozen by the incessant noise of the transmissions and by the automatic but inexplicably halting machine, are not human beings: nobody greets them, nobody apologizes for bumping into them; if they are called to do some small task, they carry it out but immediately return to their machine; they are shown what to do by a jerk of the head; they stand there in their petticoats, subjected to the pettiest power, and have not even enough calm good sense to acknowledge and conciliate that power by their looks and gestures.

Kafka commented in his diary about how the female employees in his brother-in-law's factory were dehumanized by their mechanical work. This 1909 Lewis Hine photograph shows young women working in a box factory in Tampa, Florida.

• • • • •

This piping which rises up, when all others are enjoined to silence, comes almost as a message from the people to each individual; the thin piping of Josefine in the midst of grave decisions is almost like the pitiful existence of our people amid the tumult of the hostile world.

"Josefine" is not about Zionism, nor, despite some hints, can the mice be unequivocally identified with the Jewish people. It puts forward a conception of a community, repeatedly using the word Volk (*people*), which in German suggests intense solidarity based on natural bonds, and even *Volksgenosse* (fellow-member of the people), a word that was harmless in 1924 but has since been discredited through having been misused by ideologists of the Right. Kafka's use of it does not place him on the political Right but shows that the vision of social solidarity found here and there in his works does not correspond to the conventional political opposition between Right and Left.

In *The Castle* society is treated much more skeptically. Although the village may present a united front to outsiders such as K., internally it is riven by factions, and it quickly ostracizes anyone, such as the Barnabas family, who appears to break with traditional customs. Toward the Castle, seat of their feudal overlord and his bureaucratic representatives, the villagers are trapped in a relationship of authority and submission. The way out of such a relationship offered in the text is through marriage. On his second day in the village K. takes up with Frieda, the barmaid at the Bridge Inn, spends the night with her, and thereafter describes her as his fiancée. But there is the obvious danger that marriage to Frieda could simply reproduce the familiar structure of authority, with a patriarchal husband dominating an acquiescent wife. Kafka had experienced that structure at home, in the primordial institution of the family. In his diary and letters, his father typically shouts and his mother "whimpers." In Kafka's lifetime, however, opportunities for women to gain independence and realize their potential increased sharply. During the first decade of the twentieth century, women were gradually admitted to university in the various German states, Prussia being last in 1909. In Austria, Vienna University admitted women to its arts faculty in 1897, and to the study of medicine in 1900. More and more women were taking jobs. Kafka's female friends represented the New Woman type. Felice, having begun work as a shorthand typist, had within four years become chief clerk of her firm (*Prokurist*, the post occupied by Josef K.). Her friend Grete Bloch, who for a while mediated between Kafka and Felice, had a similar, even more successful career. Milena Jesenská was

Opportunities for women to gain independence and realize their potential increased dramatically during Kafka's lifetime, such as at previously male-only educational institutions. This photochrom print of Vienna University was created between 1890 and 1900, around the time that women were first admitted to its faculty and student body.

Kafka and his sister Ottla, 1914.

a noted journalist. Kafka's favorite sister Ottla worked on a country estate and later attended an agricultural college.

Such types appear also in Kafka's fiction. Fräulein Bürstner in *The Trial*, who works as a secretary in a legal firm, is an independent professional woman. Both her landlady and the old-fashioned Josef K. suspect her of sexual immorality and availability. Her resistance to K.'s harassment establishes a contrast with the seductive, whorish women who make up to him: the wife of the Court servant, who declares provocatively, "You can do anything you like with me," and the housekeeper Leni who lures him away from a discussion of his lawsuit. While *The Trial* thus gives a familiar binary opposition between the chaste and the sexualized woman, *The Castle* shows much greater differentiation in its portrayal of women. It presents us with a range of highly developed female characters, reflecting not only the possibilities open to women but also the images of women available in Kafka's lifetime.

In *The Castle* the New Woman is represented rather unappealingly by the schoolteacher Gisa. Imperious, gimlet-eyed, she dominates her lover Schwarzer, who is so submissive that he spends his time with her helping her to correct school exercises. Gisa, however, does not really want a relationship and is happiest when she can stretch herself out on her sofa in the company of her cat.

A more traditional female role is represented by Gardena, the landlady of the Bridge Inn, who feels dissatisfied with her relatively youthful husband, not least because she is still under the spell of her brief relationship with Klamm eighteen years earlier. This attraction to Klamm illustrates a kind of romanticism which simply spoils her present life and which K. tries to persuade her to abandon. In her feminist reading of Kafka, Elizabeth Boa interprets these romantic longings as a device that keeps women imprisoned in the patriarchal order of the village and its subsystem, the matriarchal order of the home. In practice, however, such romantic yearnings seem to be an obstacle to the acceptance of everyday life, a female correlative to K.'s destructive obsession with the Castle. The same obsession traps Olga in promiscuous sexual activity with Castle servants and Amalia in the well-known role of caring for her aged and increasingly feeble parents.

Finally, there is Frieda, who is briefly engaged to K. The account of their relationship is the closest Kafka comes to a fictional portrayal of marriage. Marriage is here conceived in a characteristically modern way as a relationship between equals which is strenuous and challenging, a psychological testing ground on which many—including K. and Frieda—fail. This is a new conception. The older conception of marriage as the assigning to husband and wife of separate tasks (professional and domestic) still governs such nineteenth-century novels as *Madame Bovary*, in which Emma is bored by her dull husband and her limited opportunities, and *Middlemarch*, which shows Dorothea frustrated in her hopes of serving her husband's work as his amanuensis. The more challenging conception of marriage was inaugurated by Ibsen, whose plays undercut conventional images of masculinity by showing the men as weak, selfish, and self-deceived, and transfer the focus to the women and their dissatisfaction with their

Kafka admired Swedish playwright and novelist August Strindberg (1849–1912), shown here in a photograph taken ca. 1890–1900, and Kafka's close reading of the playwright's work is evident in his portrayal of the relationship between K. and Frieda in *The Castle*.

relationships. In *A Doll's House*, *Hedda Gabler*, and that searing marital drama *Little Eyolf*, marriage is an arena in which emotional differences, once confronted, either wreck the marriage or lead through a crisis to a new relationship. Ibsen's contemporary and counterpart, Strindberg, whose work Kafka intensely admired, shows marriage in his autobiography, fiction, and drama as a battleground in which the woman has the upper hand. In Ibsen and Strindberg, and soon afterward in D. H. Lawrence, marriage takes the place of adventure in the chivalric romance, and of work in the nineteenth-century novel, as the setting where character develops through conflict.

The relationship between Frieda and K. elicits a poignancy rare in Kafka. Although K. does initially imagine using her as a means of approaching Klamm, he finds himself loving her for her own sake, and the growth and fading of their love is evoked in lyrical passages whose tone has not previously appeared in Kafka's work. The first of these occurs, unexpectedly, in the sexual encounter between K. and Frieda. Initially Frieda may seem like another version of the woman as vampiric temptress. She wields a whip, faintly suggesting the terrifying women of earlier stories (though here the whip serves to control the brutish servants who are carrying Olga off to the stable), and she pulls K. down to the floor, like Leni in *The Trial*. Yet despite the disgusting setting on the filthy barroom floor, the experience sidetracks K. from his single-minded campaign against the Castle, breaks down his masculine defenses, and brings him close to Frieda, as is underlined by the repetition of "as one":

> There hours passed, hours of breathing as one, hearts beating as one, hours in which K. constantly had the feeling that he had lost his way or wandered farther into a strange land than anyone before him, a strange land where even the air held no trace of the air at home, where a man must suffocate from the strangeness yet into whose foolish enticements he could do nothing but plunge on, getting even more lost.

Although the relationship between K. and Frieda is short-lived, its various episodes—meeting, setting up house in the schoolroom, wrangling, and estrangement—amount to a telescoped narrative of a marriage and its breakdown. The variety of feeling evoked in Kafka's account of their relationship suggests both reflection on his own experience and thorough reading of Strindberg's portrayals of marriage. Frieda's love is a spontaneous gift, for which she hides K. from the Landlord and defends him against the disapproval of the Landlady. But it also has something deadly and constricting in it, as is evident when she imagines being together with K. in a shared grave:

> when I dream, I really do, that there's no quiet place here on earth for our love, not in the village and not anywhere else, so I picture a grave deep and narrow, in which we embrace as if clamped together, I bury my face against you, you yours against me, and no one will ever see us again.

On K.'s side, both his irritation and his egocentricity during their marital arguments are skillfully conveyed. When Frieda begins to reproach him, he is more annoyed than touched by her lamenting voice, "even finding the tearfully plaintive voice more irritating than moving." On another occasion, when Frieda tells him how much she needs and wants him, K. ignores her touching appeal and picks up only a reference to Klamm:

> "You think I miss Klamm?" said Frieda, "there's a surfeit of Klamm here, too much Klamm; it's to escape him that I want to get away. I don't miss Klamm, I miss you. It's because of you I want to leave; because I can't get enough of you, with everyone tugging at me here. I'd rather the pretty mask were torn away, I'd rather my body were wretched, so I might live in peace with you." K. heard only one thing in all this. "Klamm's still in touch with you?" he asked promptly, "he sends for you?"

The marital relationship founders, perhaps on Frieda's possessiveness, certainly on K.'s egotism. The institution of marriage, as a partnership between equals requiring each to emerge from his or her solitary obsessions, appears here as a Utopia, something glimpsed only in the moment of its failure. However precarious, it represents in Kafka a tentative counterideal to the family as he had known it, the potential nucleus of a new society not founded on authority and submission.

FIVE

The Last Things

•

When I try to put all into a phrase I say: "Man can embody truth but he cannot know it."

W. B. Yeats

"Where Is God Gone?"

Kafka's approach to religion may be indicated by juxtaposing two passages. One, "The Trees," comes from his early book *Meditation*. The other is a famous passage from Nietzsche.

For we are like the trunks of trees in the snow. Apparently they rest smoothly on the surface and with a gentle push we should

Kafka likened people to the seemingly movable trees in the snow. This photochrom print was made as part of a collection of travel views of Europe between 1890 and 1900.

be able to shift them. No, that one cannot, for they are firmly attached to the ground. But see, that too is only apparent.

"Where is God gone?" he cried, "I will tell you! We have killed him—you and I! All of us are his murderers! But how did we do this. How were we able to drink up the sea? Who gave us the sponge to wipe away the whole horizon? What were we doing when we unchained this earth from its sun? Where is it going now? Where are we going? Away from all suns? Are we not continually plunging? And backwards, sideways, forwards, in all directions? Is there still an above and a below? Are we not wandering through an infinite nothingness? Don't we feel the breath of empty space? Has it not grown colder? Doesn't night and more night keep coming? Must not lanterns be lighted in the morning? Do we yet hear nothing of the noise of the grave-diggers who are burying God? (Nietzsche, *The Joyful Wisdom*, 125)

There is a great difference in tone between these two passages. Kafka's meditation is quiet and enigmatic. Nietzsche's is a dramatic utterance ascribed to a madman, trying to make the sane realize the enormity of their situation. But both express how the world has lost any secure foundation. Trees growing out of the snow seem to be standing upon it and easy to push away. In fact they resist our attempts to move them: they seem far more firmly rooted than we are. But this rootedness is—in some sense which the parable invites us to supply—only illusory. Even the seemingly most solid objects lack any unshakeable foundation. In Nietzsche, this lack of foundation results from the death of God: not simply from disbelief in him, but from humanity's rebellious assumption of control over our own lives. Thanks to our violent denial of God, the world has lost the clear shape, the firm horizon, the stable foundation that it formerly possessed. There are no reference points anymore, no above and below, and we cannot stop the earth from careering into darkness, any more than we can control or imagine the consequences once humanity has rejected God's tutelage.

Kafka repeatedly evokes the situation in which a source of authority is, or has become, inaccessibly remote. Thus in "A Message from the Emperor" (published in *A Country Doctor*) the emperor has sent the addressee a message from his deathbed, but the messenger, though strong and even "indefatigable," has to force his way through the royal palace, and the inner chambers, the stairs, the courtyards, the outer palace, each representing a space so vast that he can never force his way through it and can never bring you the message from the dead emperor. "But," the story concludes, "you sit at your window and dream up that message when evening falls." Even if God is dead, we want a divine message, and if none is available we will imagine it for ourselves.

In Kafka's novels the declining or absent authority is often figured in religious imagery. In *The Man Who Disappeared*, the ultramodern New York still has a cathedral whose form looms out of a haze, but in Pollunder's country house the chapel appears to have been abandoned as part of the modernization of the building. The Cathedral in *The Trial* is huge, dark, almost deserted, and of interest to Josef K. primarily as a tourist attraction. A painting of Christ being laid in the tomb, which K. can make out only piecemeal with the aid of his pocket flashlight, ceases to interest him when he identifies it as a recent picture. The darkness of the Cathedral recalls another saying of Nietzsche's madman: "What are these churches now, if not the tombs and monuments of God?" In

Kafka's last novel, the Castle is explicitly contrasted with the church of K.'s hometown:

> And he drew a mental comparison between the church tower of his hometown and the tower above him. The tower at home, neatly, unhesitatingly tapering straight upward, ending below in a red-tiled expanse of roof, an earthly building—what other kind can we build?—yet with a loftier goal than the squat jumble of houses and making a clearer statement than the drab working day.

The Castle, on the other hand, is indistinct and puzzling:

> On the whole, seen from this distance, the castle matched K.'s expectations. It was neither an old-style knight's stronghold, nor a modern palace, but an extended complex consisting of a few two-storied but a great many lower buildings set close together; had you not known it was a castle, you might have taken it for a small town. K. saw only one tower, there was no telling whether it belonged to a residential building or to a church.

How does the Castle match K.'s expectations if it does not look like a castle? And how did he know in advance that it was a castle? On closer inspection, it reveals itself as really "just a wretched-looking small town, a collection of rustic hovels." Although situated high above the village, it looks scarcely different from the village: a hint perhaps that nowadays the authority to which people submit is conceived in their own image.

Kafka's frequent reference to churches testifies to the Christian atmosphere in which he lived: not in his Jewish family, but in Prague, a city dominated by massive churches. Kafka sometimes dates diary entries by reference to Christian festivals (Easter Saturday, Corpus Christi), since these were public holidays. Christianity was readily available to him as a cultural system. Its appearance in his fiction, however, is hard to interpret. In *The Judgment*, Georg and his friend suggest the Prodigal Son and his stay-at-home brother. "Petersburg," the city of Peter, recalls St. Peter and Rome. We have the striking and at first sight unmotivated image of the priest in Russia who stands up before a crowd and cuts a cross into the palm of his hand. After sentence has been pronounced, the maidservant cries "Jesus!" as Georg dashes downstairs to his fate, and hides her face as though the sight of him were forbidden. Hanging from the bridge, Georg may call to mind the crucified Christ. In *The Transformation*, Gregor, assailed by his father with apples, feels "as if nailed to the spot," again like Christ on the cross. The victim suffering on the punishment machine of *In the Penal Colony* gains enlightenment "at the sixth hour." The sick boy in "A Country Doctor," watched by two horses, seems to be reversing the birth of Christ in the stable. The Fasting Artist starves for forty days, like Christ in the wilderness.

Enigmatic as these allusions are, they often imply a criticism of the values of Christianity. As a reader of Nietzsche, Kafka was undoubtedly familiar with the critique of religion in general, and Christianity in particular, found throughout Nietzsche's writings. Nietzsche denied that the moral and theological claims of Christianity had any divine origin. There was no single morality, but rather diverse systems of morals, whose origin could be explained historically and psychologically, and whose dominance was due not to their intrinsic excellence but to the power attained by their adherents. Christian morality

Kafka grew up in Prague, a city dominated by its massive churches. Shown here is a ca. 1890 photograph of a bird's-eye view of Prague, with church spires accenting the cityscape.

represented the creative resentment felt by the physically weak against their masters, and was shot through with vengefulness and hatred. The priestly type, best realized in Judaism and Christianity, was a damaged person, lacking in vitality, maintaining power over his sick flock by psychological manipulation. Though Jesus had a valuable message, only a natural aristocracy could have understood it, whereas his disciples were mediocre individuals and St. Paul a fanatical nihilist who distorted the message to satisfy his power hunger. And yet Nietzsche acknowledged that the slave revolt in morals which produced Christianity had also made humanity more inward, more complex, more interesting, and that the asceticism exemplified by the priest was shared by the artist and the scholar, in whom it was the precondition for achievement. In this light, Kafka's self-mutilating priest in *The Judgment* may be seen as a version of the sick priest in *The Genealogy of Morals*, who owes his power over his flock to his sharing their illness. The selfish family in *The Transformation* cross themselves when they learn, to their relief, that Gregor is dead. Johanna Brummer, the maidservant who abuses Karl in *The Man Who Disappeared*, prays to a wooden crucifix. The Country Doctor reflects that his patients have transferred their superstitious faith from the useless priest to him:

> They have lost their old faith; the priest sits at home and picks
> his vestments to pieces, one by one; but the doctor is expected to
> accomplish everything with his sensitive surgical hand.

Kafka was aware that medical treatment could invite as much credulity as religious cults. After hearing a speaker denounce the superstition surrounding the shrine at Lourdes, Kafka reflected in his diary:

Karlsbad [a famous health resort, now Karlovy vary] is a bigger swindle than Lourdes, and Lourdes has the advantage that people go there because of their deepest faith. What about rigid opinions concerning operations, serum cures, injections, medicines?

Kafka's Jewish upbringing, and his renewal of interest in aspects of Jewish culture and religion from about 1911, might be expected to leave deeper traces in his work. Admittedly, he complained to his father of

Kafka compared Karlsbad unfavorably to Lourdes, calling them both a swindle. Both these photochrom prints, showing Lourdes Grotto (top), near the nunnery of Ingenbohl, in Lake Lucerne, Switzerland, and the Muhl Spring (bottom) at Karlsbad (now Karlovy Vary, in the Czech Republic) were created between 1890 and 1900.

having been introduced only to a shallow and desultory form of Judaism, characteristic of Jews moving from tight rural communities to the cities where traditional allegiances became diluted. His father went to the synagogue only on the High Holidays. At the age of thirteen, Kafka had a bar mitzvah which his parents, in a concession to the dominant Christianity typical of assimilated Jews, called "confirmation"; he remembered laboriously learning by heart a prayer which he recited in the synagogue, and then delivering a prepared speech at home. The first night of Passover was celebrated in the Kafka household, but taken less and less seriously. After attending the circumcision of his nephew in 1911, Kafka reflected that the ceremony, watched uncomprehendingly by most of those present, was so obviously a historic survival that it would soon acquire historical interest. Reacting against his family's disapproval of Jews from Poland and Russia, Kafka learned much about Eastern Jewish culture from the Yiddish actors whose performances he attended loyally in 1911–12, and he later he became friendly with Georg Langer, a Czech-speaking Prague Jew who told him much about the Kabbalah (the medieval tradition of Jewish mysticism) and the Baal Shem who founded the religious revival movement known as Hasidism in the early eighteenth century; Langer had himself lived in the Hasidic community of Belz, near the Russian frontier, and in Marienbad in 1916 he and Kafka saw the Rabbi of Belz, who had come there with his followers to take refuge from Russian armies. Kafka read the Hasidic stories translated and reworked by Martin Buber, and treasured a pocket anthology from the Talmud.

How far all this Jewish lore entered Kafka's fiction is difficult to say. Though churches often feature, a synagogue is mentioned only in a short fragment ("In the Thamühl Synagogue"). Jewish imagery sometimes appears more discreetly. A few months before beginning

The Trial, Kafka visited Martin Buber in Berlin and asked him about the "unjust judges" in Psalm 82. Many intriguing similarities have been pointed out between the imagery of the novel and that of the Kabbalah, with its judges and doorkeepers, though it is not clear how much Kafka knew about the Kabbalah at this stage in his life. It was noted many years ago, by Evelyn Torton Beck, that the Hebrew word for "land surveyor," K.'s profession in *The Castle*, resembles that for "messiah," suggesting another aspect of K.'s intrusion into the village. *The Judgment* was written during the night following Yom Kippur, when Kafka had failed to attend synagogue, and after a year of absorption in the full-blooded Jewish life represented by the Yiddish actors from Warsaw who were visiting Prague. Many biblical allusions have been surmised in the story. The "nightmare image of his father" suggests an angry Jehovah, a reminder of the authority of tradition, who punishes Georg for his apostasy into worldly pursuits. Georg and his friend, implicitly made into brothers when the father says of the friend: "He would

Kafka, whose work has been linked to Jewish mysticism, though there is no definitive evidence that he was well versed in the subject, went to visit Jewish philosopher Martin Buber, shown here in a photograph taken in 1962, in Berlin to ask him about the judges in Psalm 82 shortly before beginning his work on *The Trial*.

have been a son after my own heart," faintly recall such contrasting Old Testament pairs as Jacob and Esau, or Ephraim and Manasseh (Gen. 48). However, such interpretations impute to Kafka a degree of conscious planning which is hardly compatible with the way he wrote the story or with the perplexity he himself expressed about it, and a thorough knowledge of Jewish theology and tradition, which is not attested in any contemporary biographical documents.

Despite these difficulties, some of Kafka's most eminent Jewish interpreters have found in his work a profound response to and revision of specifically Jewish themes. The philosopher Margarete Susman (1872–1966) saw Kafka in 1929 as addressing the problem of Job, who questions God's justice, but in the modern secularized world from which God seems to be absent.

> If the world of mechanized work, purely functional work devoid of sense and soul, were suddenly invaded by the law of God—if the living creation itself demanded its rights: then the world would look as Kafka depicts it.

Five years later, the religious interpretation of *The Trial* was debated in letters between the critic Walter Benjamin and the scholar and theologian Gershom Scholem (now recognized as a towering figure not only in the study of the Kabbalah but in modern German-Jewish thought). Benjamin, repelled by the facile religious interpretations advanced by Max Brod and others, maintained that Kafka's imagination had gone back before the beginnings of religion and regained contact with the prehistoric thought-world out of which religion was to develop. Scholem countered that Kafka did indeed depict the world in the light of divine revelation, but it was a revelation that could not be fulfilled, because its message could not be deciphered. And Scholem, in his letter of July 9, 1934, expressed his understanding of Kafka as the bearer of a negative theology in a remarkable poem which unfortunately defies verse-translation, beginning:

Are we quite cut off from You? In such a night, God, is not a breath of Your peace and Your message destined for us?

Can Your word have died away so completely in the emptiness of Zion—or never penetrated into this magic realm of semblance?

The world's great deception is wellnigh consummated and complete. Grant, God, that the man pierced by Your nothingness may awaken.

Only thus can revelation shine into the age that rejected You. Your nothingness is the only way it can know You.

Whatever Kafka's relation to Jewish thought, he was increasingly preoccupied with questions of religion. This does not mean his allegiance to any specific religion, whether Judaism, Christianity, or any variety thereof. His reading in religion and philosophy was wide and eclectic. From 1917 onward, when his extended spells off work gave him ample time for reading, he read Pascal, Schopenhauer, the *Confessions* of St. Augustine, the Christian diaries of the late Tolstoy, and much else. He paid particular attention to Kierkegaard, and it is often supposed that the Danish religious philosopher provides some kind of key to Kafka's works. Brod, especially, encouraged this notion in his afterword to *The Castle*. The facts of Kafka's reception of Kierkegaard, however, suggest a somewhat different picture.

Kafka first read Kierkegaard in 1913. He read a selection from Kierkegaard's journals published as *Buch des Richters* (*Book of the Judge*) and found that his own conflict between marriage to Felice and commitment to writing strongly resembled the conflict Kierkegaard felt between marriage and the religious commitment which led him to break off his engagement to Regine Olsen. He returned to Kierkegaard's works in 1917–18 and discussed them in letters to Brod. Kafka seems to have been particularly impressed by *Fear and Trembling*, an extended meditation

This **chiaroscuro** woodcut of *The Sacrifice of Abraham* was created between ca. 1520 and 1700 by an anonymous artist after Francesco Mazzuoli.

on the story of Abraham and Isaac. Kierkegaard is interested in how the religious life not only lies beyond the ethical life, but may contradict it. A person may, in the service of God, do things that are utterly repugnant to morality. Thus God commanded Abraham to sacrifice his first-born son, whereupon Abraham obediently took the boy up to Mount Moriah and prepared to kill him; at the last moment he saw a ram caught in a thicket which God, relenting, had sent as a substitute. Abraham put his obedience to God before his moral sense, his fatherly affection, and the ethical standards of his society. To Kafka, this showed that religious belief was an utterly individual, private matter, which only God could judge. "For the relationship to the divine, for Kierkegaard, is removed from any other person's judgment, so much perhaps that even Jesus could not judge how far someone who follows him has come," he wrote to Brod in March 1918.

Something of this ethical individualism appears in *The Castle*. Brod maintained that Sortini's obscene summons to Amalia was analogous to God's apparently immoral command to Abraham, and that Amalia, unlike Abraham, erred by rejecting it. This interpretation is not self-evident and is not borne out by any of Kafka's com-

Kafka first began to read the work of Søren Kierkegaard (1813–55) in 1913. The Danish philosopher and theologian is shown here in *Søren Kierkegaard at His High Desk*, an oil on canvas by Danish artist Luplau Janssen.

ments. Rather, the individualism that enables K. to challenge the Castle and defy local traditions seems connected with a passage that Kafka, in the same letter to Brod, quotes from the *Book of the Judge*:

As soon as a person appears who has something primitive about him, so that he does not say "One must accept the world as it is" [. . .] but says "However the world is, I shall retain an originality which I do not mean to alter in accordance with the world's wishes": at the moment these words are heard, the whole of existence is transformed. As in the fairy-tale, when the word is spoken, the castle opens after being enchanted for a hundred years, and everything comes to life: so existence turns into sheer attention.

A person who has retained his original character—the "individuality" of which, Kafka complained, parents and educators sought to deprive one—arouses the attention both of angels and of demons, opening up possibilities of extreme good or evil.

Reading Kierkegaard helped Kafka to see his own experience in a wider perspective, as shared by at least one other person, and in a religious framework. The insecurity that we have seen documented in previous chapters sought support in something outside human life, and his devotion to writing became more than literature, more than self-therapy, pointing the way to a justification for his existence. In 1913 he asked Felice about her belief in God and enlarged on the conception he thought desirable:

> Do you feel—this is the main thing—unbroken connections between yourself and some reassuringly remote, possibly infinite, height or depth? Anyone who constantly feels that does not have to run around like a lost dog, looking around beseechingly but mutely, he need not feel the desire to slip into the grave as though it were a warm sleeping-bag and life a cold winter night, and when he climbs the stairs to his office, he does not have to think he sees himself simultaneously falling from above down the entire staircase, shimmering in the uncertain light, revolving with the rapidity of his motion, shaking his head with impatience.

This is a brilliant evocation of existential insecurity. Similarly, Kafka's need to write becomes existential, religious, when it provides a justification for his existence. While working on *The Trial*, he wrote in his diary:

> I am not so fully protected, so curled up in my work, as I was two years ago [thinking back to the composition of *The Judgment*], still, I have found a meaning, my regular, empty, mad, bachelor-like life has a justification.

As Kafka came to understand his life situation in religious terms, he rejected psychoanalytic explanations. He knew a good deal about various schools of psychoanalysis, largely from discussion and from reading articles about it in the *New Review* and elsewhere. He noted that while writing *The Judgment* he had had "thoughts about Freud, naturally." But he felt that psychoanalysis gave facile explanations which were intensely satisfying at first but soon left one has hungry as before—though of course psychoanalysis could itself explain this response as repression of the

Kafka said he thought about Austrian psychoanalyst Sigmund Freud as he composed *The Judgment* but felt that the claims of psychoanalysis that it cured people's neuroses were dehumanizing. The founder of psychoanalysis is shown here in a photograph taken in 1926 by portrait artist Ferdinand Schmutzer.

unwelcome truth. Above all, he thought that the claims of psycho-analysis to cure people of their neuroses were dehumanizing. In a letter to Brod he quoted a sentence from Kierkegaard as being relevant to Freud: "No human being can lead a true spiritual life while remaining perfectly healthy in body and mind." And to Milena, who had evidently found his insecurity baffling, he replied:

> Try to understand it by calling it illness. It is one of the many symptoms of illness which psychoanalysis claims to have discovered. I do not call it illness and see the therapeutic part of psychoanalysis as a helpless error. All these so-called illnesses, however sad they may look, are facts of faith, where a human being in distress anchors himself in some maternal soil.

When such attempts to anchor oneself found a real foundation, he continued, they were not to be seen as contingent features of one's life but part of human nature and hence not something that should be "cured."

"To Become Clear About the Last Things"

The later Kafka seeks a solid foundation and a justification for his own life, and for that of others. He comes to see himself as representing the spiritual situation of his time. A notebook entry dated February 25, 1918, presents him as confronted with a mysterious spiritual task:

> I have brought none of life's requirements, so far as I know, but only universal human weakness. With this—in this respect it is gigantic strength—I have powerfully absorbed the negative aspect

of my age, which is very close to me, which I have no right to combat but in a certain sense to represent. I had no inherited share in the scanty positive aspect nor in the extreme negative that turns into the positive. I was not led into life by the sinking hand of Christianity, like Kierkegaard, nor did I catch the tip of the Jewish prayer-shawl as it flew away, like the Zionists. I am the end or the beginning.

This sense of personal crisis and personal mission as representative of his age comes late in a long series of notebook entries made during the winter of 1917–18 at Zürau in the Bohemian countryside, where Kafka, now diagnosed as tubercular, was staying with his sister and convalescing from his hemorrhage. He told Brod, on a visit to Prague that December, what his task was: "To become clear about the last things. The Western Jew is not clear about them and therefore has no right to marry." Detached from a religious tradition which was rapidly vanishing into history, the Western Jew lacked guidance about the "last things" (curiously, a Christian term, customarily understood to mean heaven, hell, death, and judgment, but evidently used here in a wider and looser sense) and therefore lacked the spiritual support necessary before one assumed the awesome responsibility of marrying and starting a family. For Kafka, his difficulties over marrying Felice have by now come to typify the spiritual benightedness of the assimilated and secularized Western Jew. In thinking through the spiritual bases of human life, he is acting not just for himself but for the community to which he belongs. The aphorisms in the Zürau notebooks are a coherent body of religious meditations, vivid, sharply formulated, often witty, and endlessly thought-provoking. In 1921 Kafka arranged a selection from them

Kafka died of tuberculosis in 1924 at the age of forty. His gravestone is in the Jewish cemetery in Prague.

in a numbered series, to which Max Brod, finding them after Kafka's death, gave the title "Reflections on Sin, Suffering, Hope, and the True Way." They deserve detailed discussion to show Kafka's preeminence as, among much else, a religious thinker.

The aphorisms are first and foremost the expression of a spiritual crisis. One finds oneself in a situation that cannot be resolved, not just because the solution is impossibly difficult, but because the solution is unimaginable. "You are the problem. No scholar far and wide"—in an impossible act of self-reflexivity, one is required to solve a puzzle, to do a piece of homework, that is nothing other than oneself. In this situation, one feels driven to make the crisis more desperate, to reach the point of no return. "From a certain point there is no longer any return. This point must be reached." When the crisis is at its most extreme, hope may emerge, as another aphorism suggests: "The true antagonist fills you with boundless courage."

The situation that Kafka is writing about, in general rather than personal terms, is first of all one of self-estrangement. Our consciousness, our cognitive apparatus, cannot know about our true being and therefore serves to estrange us from ourselves and from the truth. The problem is not that one cannot know the truth; it is that one cannot know the truth and *be* the truth: "There are only two things: the truth and the lie. The truth is indivisible, so cannot know itself. Anyone who seeks to know it must be [a] lie."

For Kafka, the contemplation of life is bound to be deceptive. This is partly because the signs of the world are ambiguous. "The man in ecstasy and the man drowning: both raise their arms": the same gesture can have opposite meanings. "All is deception." But that is also because our powers of perception are inadequate. Estranged from one's true self, one perceives everything unreliably. One cannot know oneself. "Only evil has self-knowledge." One cannot know anything else, because either one is involved and hence biased, or else one is neutral and hence ignorant: "Only the party concerned can really judge, but as a party concerned s/he cannot judge. Hence the world contains no possibility of judgment, only its semblance."

The task of the individual, as Kafka sees it, is to resist the world. But how is one to do that if one cannot know anything for certain about the world? Worse still, since one is estranged from oneself, it may be that the self from which one is estranged is in league with the world. And that is bound to be the case in so far as estrangement divides the mind from the body. For with our bodies we are enmeshed in the world of the senses, which Kafka considers at best illusory, at worst evil. "There is nothing but a spiritual world; what we call the sensory world is the evil in the spiritual [world]." To fight against the sensory world is futile, because one's senses, and especially one's sexuality, are complicit with it. "One of the most effective temptations practiced by the devilish [element] is the invitation to a fight. It is like the fight with women, which ends up in bed." The struggle against the world is especially a struggle against sexuality:

> Woman—to put it more pointedly, perhaps, marriage—is the representative of life with which you are to struggle. The means by which this world tempts you, and the sign guaranteeing that this world is only transitional, are the same. Rightly so, for it is only thus that the world could tempt us, corresponding to the truth. The bad thing is only that after the temptation has worked, we forget the guarantee, and so it is really the good that has lured us into evil, the woman's gaze has lured us into her bed.

Although love—not just sensual love, but the element of heavenly love within it—keeps us trapped in the sensual world, Kafka regards the soul as something eternal, temporarily confined within the physical world. "I am too confined in everything I signify; even the eternity that I am confines me too much." The soul, it seems, is conceived as disembodied, almost abstract.

How is one to escape from this confinement? First, one must become aware of one's condition. This leads to despair. "A first sign of the beginning of knowledge is the wish to die. This life seems unendurable, another [life] unattainable." But becoming aware of one's condition is not enough, for mere self-knowledge is a distraction from the necessary task of overcoming the world. Instead, one's motto must be: "Fail to know yourself! Destroy yourself!"—and only when one stoops very far down can one hear the good part, which runs: "in order to make yourself into that which you are." Kafka demands active self-destruction. One must die, but not a physical death. "Our salvation is death, but not this one." Rather, one must undergo a spiritual death, and the only development Kafka sees in human history is the development of this spiritual power: "Humanity's development—a growth of the power to die." He represents spiritual death by the image of the burning bush in which the Lord appeared to Moses in Exodus 3:2.

This stained-glass representation of Moses and the burning bush is in Notre-Dame de Laon, a twelfth–thirteenth-century Gothic cathedral in Laon, Picardy, France.

"The thorn-bush is the ancient barrier in the road. It must catch fire if you want to go any further." Spiritual progress must be through the fire, an image recalling Purgatory. Kafka, however, adopts the Jewish image of the Holy of Holies:

> Before entering the Holy of Holies you must take off your shoes, and not only your shoes but everything, your traveling clothes and your baggage, and beneath that your nakedness, and everything that is beneath your nakedness, and everything hidden beneath that, and then the core and the core of the core, then what is left and then the rest and then the light from the imperishable fire.

Having undergone such self-destruction, such purgation, what new reality may the purified self enter? Kafka talks mysteriously of our life as being merely transitional. We need to enter the spiritual world, which is the only reality.

> There is nothing but a spiritual world; what we call the sensuous world is the evil in the spiritual [world], and what we call evil is only a requirement of a moment in our everlasting development.

Our mission is "ascent into a higher life," indeed to attain eternal life.

> If, having gained knowledge, you want to attain eternal life—and you cannot do other than want to, for knowledge is this desire— then you will have to destroy yourself, the obstacle.

So far we have a sharp division between the world of the senses, which one's body inhabits, and the spiritual world of eternity to which one is connected by one's bodiless inner, or mental, self. Some passages remind us strongly of Kafka's personal revulsion from sexuality which makes him in his notebooks equate marriage with martyrdom. There is, however, a countercurrent in Kafka's thought: the idea that possibly the world of the senses can after all be made acceptable. He contemplates this possibility at first with something approaching horror:

> What is depressing about the idea of eternity: the incomprehensible justification that time must receive in eternity and the consequent justification of ourselves, just as we are.

Suppose our destiny were not to escape from embodied existence into a higher, nonphysical reality, but to see our limited, temporal reality as part of the eternal order and having its rightful place in the eternal order. Granted that the sensory world is the evil element in the spiritual world, perhaps even this can be reclaimed. A Christian would say "redeemed"; Kafka's word is "justification," and as this is an important word in the notebooks the concept deserves some attention. In the Old Testament, this word expresses a relationship between human beings and God. The man who is justified is acquitted or vindicated before a judge's tribunal, as in Psalm 119:7: "I will praise thee with uprightness of heart, when I shall have learned thy righteous judgments." St. Paul transfers this concept to the work of Christ, thanks to whom, not to any merits or actions of our own, we are justified, found righteous, before God: while Abraham was justified by his faith ("And therefore it was imputed to him for righteousness," Rom. 4:22), Christians are justified both by faith in Christ and by the death of Christ for their sake: "Therefore being justified by faith, we have peace with God through our Lord Jesus Christ" (Rom. 5:1).

As Kafka develops the concept, however, justification does not come from an external source. It comes from man's own work in the world. Man does not consciously seek justification:

> That it appears as though he were working to feed and clothe himself, etc., does not matter; for with every visible mouthful he also receives an invisible one, with every visible dress he also receives an invisible dress. That is everybody's justification.

A person who concentrates on working to support himself and his family is already justified without consciously knowing it. In such a person, being and consciousness are reconciled. Such a person, like the family Flaubert envied, is "*dans le vrai*." We can relate this conception to *The Castle*. There K. seeks a justification for his presence in the village. He wants the authorities to confirm his position as land surveyor. In his search for authorization, he becomes obsessed with the Castle and with his need to speak to an official competent to deal with his case. Early in this process, he takes up with Frieda, the girlfriend of the official Klamm, and they stumble into a relationship which both want to be lasting. K. finds work as a school janitor, and maintains a grotesquely impractical household in the schoolroom. It is not the difficulties of daily life, but the lure of the Castle, which ends his relationship with Frieda.

A further aphorism explores the basis of this justification. It is based on faith, not in the sense of conscious belief, but in the sense of trust, an unconscious assurance, which pervades one's whole being.

> Man cannot live without lasting trust in something indestructible, even if in lasting ignorance both of his trust and of the indestructible. One possible expression of this concealment is the belief in a personal God.

Here Kafka affirms that life needs to be based on a relationship to something outside oneself. He is skeptical about whether that something should be conceived as a personal God. But we have already seen how between 1913 and 1917 Kafka's insecurity had reached the point of desperation. He worked through his crisis in the Zürau notebooks. There he formulates the concept of "the indestructible," derived from Schopenhauer's famous meditation on death in *The World as Will and Idea* (see sidebar on page 154).

Belief in "the indestructible" is not intellectual. It is expressed in action. "Belief means freeing the indestructible in oneself, or rather: freeing oneself, or rather: being indestructible, or rather: being." It bridges the gulf between consciousness and being. And it enables Kafka effortlessly to surmount a problem that worries many people who reflect on religion, namely the fact that the majority of people feel no need to reflect on religion. William James in *The Varieties of Religious Experience* borrows from a Catholic writer the division of humanity into the once-born and the twice-born. The latter are the minority who feel anxiety about their relation to something beyond themselves. The former are unreflective, uncomplicated, and largely content to get on with their lives. For Kafka, both classes of people arrive by different routes at the same goal, that of being; the twice-born like himself have a very much longer and more arduous journey, the others can be "*dans le vrai*" already.

Kafka's concept of "the indestructible" has further consequences. It frees the believer from isolation, for it is by definition something shared with other

· · · · ·

SCHOPENHAUER ON DEATH

All philosophers have erred in this: they place the metaphysical, the indestructible, the eternal element in man in the *intellect*. It lies exclusively in the *will*, which is entirely different from the intellect, and alone is original. [. . .] The will alone is that which conditions, the kernel of the whole phenomenon, consequently free from the forms of the phenomenon to which time belongs, thus also indestructible. Accordingly with death consciousness is certainly lost, but not that which produced and sustained consciousness; life is extinguished but not the principle of life also, which manifested itself in it. Therefore a sure feeling informs everyone that there is something in him which is absolutely imperishable and indestructible.

Arthur Schopenhauer, "On death and its relation to the indestructibility of our true nature," in The World as Will and Idea, *tr. R. B. Haldane and J. Kemp (London: Routledge and Kegan Paul, 1883), iii. 291*

· · · · ·

people. "The indestructible is one; every individual is it, and simultaneously it is common to all. Hence the extraordinarily firm unity of humanity." At this point Kafka again defines his difference from Christianity:

We too shall have to suffer all the suffering around us. Christ suffered for mankind, but mankind must suffer for Christ. We all have, not one body, but one growth, and it leads us through all pains, whether in this or that form. As the child develops through all the stages of life to old age and death—and each stage basically seems unattainable to the preceding stage, whether in desire or fear—similarly we develop—no less deeply connected with mankind than with ourselves—through all the sufferings of this world, together with all our fellow-humans. In this context there is no place for justice, but nor is there one for fear of suffering, or for the interpretation of suffering as merit.

Here Kafka relativizes the suffering of Christ. It is the task of each human being to assume Christ's role and share the suffering of the rest of humanity. And this ethical individualism, recalling what Kafka learned from Kierkegaard, is realized in common with the rest of humanity. Kafka implicitly denies St. Paul's claim that all are members of the one body (Rom. 12:5). Instead, a shared process of development overcomes the isolation of the individual and brings about the messianic age. But Kafka undermines the various significances assigned by Judaism and Christianity to the figure of the Messiah, showing that the Messiah thus becomes superfluous:

The Messiah will come once the most unbridled individualism of faith is possible, nobody destroys this possibility, nobody tolerates its destruction, and thus the graves are opened. That is perhaps also the Christian doctrine, both in the actual displaying of the example and in the symbolic displaying of the resurrection of the mediator in the individual.

There is, then, no need for a mediator like Christ to reconcile God with man. Kafka's impersonal divinity, the indestructible, is latent in every human being. To make contact with this imperishable essence is humanity's task, and when everyone does so human life will be trans-figured. As a means to this goal, suffering is necessary and valuable:

> Suffering is the positive element in this world, indeed it is the only link between this world and the positive. Only here is suffering suffering. Not as though those who suffer here are elsewhere to be elevated because of this suffering; but what in this world is called suffering, in another world, unchanged and merely freed from its opposite, is bliss.

In this hateful, prisonlike world of pain, suffering connects us with higher reality. For we suffer because we are thrust down into this world. Our discomfort here reminds us that we belong to eternity. It is not the case that, as some Christians think, we shall be rewarded for our suffering here by corresponding happiness in the next world. Rather, in the next world the spiritual potential which makes us suffer here will be freed from confinement and make us happy.

Kafka's thought hovers between several possibilities. Here he appears to contemplate a kind of spiritual rebirth which is reminiscent of the Kabbalah, with its doctrine of liberating the divine sparks that are imprisoned in the material world. But the rebirth he imagines is not located in a radically different world, but in a world that will closely resemble the present one. In *The Castle* K. appears misguided in his search for contact with the elusively higher reality of the Castle, with its absent proprietor represented by a hierarchy of bureaucrats. K.'s quest proves destructive to himself and others. It destroys the possibility of finding a place, however marginal and precarious, in the village; it wrecks his relationship with Frieda; and it thus ruins his chance of leading an ordinary, everyday life which could be in the truth ("*dans le vrai*," as Flaubert said) without any need for official legitimation from the Castle.

To acknowledge Kafka's importance as a religious thinker is essential, but also misleading. His religious thought, though coherent, is not systematic. Like Kierkegaard, he had no wish to erect a system of ideas which would give the illusion of completeness while losing contact with the uniqueness of actual experience. Hence he chose the unsystematic form of the aphorism. Moreover, Kafka's religious thought is bound up with his imaginative activity as a writer of fiction. This certainly does not mean that his fictional inventions can be read as allegorical equivalents of abstract ideas. Kafka's images are not the embodiment of preexisting concepts. Rather, both his aphorisms and his fiction are exploratory. They explore situations and themes which are among the archetypes of religious experience: guilt, despair, judgment, hope, redemption, and love. They do so by a kind of thinking in images which need be no less rigorous than thinking in concepts. They follow a logic of the imagination which engages both the intellect and the emotions of the reader. That is perhaps the source of their fascination, and a reason why Kafka's fictions, vivid yet strangely abstract, intellectual without being drily cerebral, have spoken so insistently to innumerable readers over so many decades.

REFERENCES

•

Kafka's main works are available in many translations. The following have been used here (with occasional modification):

The Trial, tr. Idris Parry (London: Penguin, 2000)

The Castle, tr. J. A. Underwood (London: Penguin, 2000)

The Man Who Disappeared (Amerika), tr. Michael Hofmann (London: Penguin, 1997)

The Transformation and Other Stories, tr. Malcolm Pasley (London: Penguin, 1992)

The Great Wall of China and Other Short Works, tr. Malcolm Pasley (London: Penguin, 1991)

The Collected Aphorisms, tr. Malcolm Pasley (London: Penguin, 1994)

See also:

The Trial: a new translation based on the restored text, tr. Breon Mitchell (New York: Schocken, 1998)

The Castle: a new translation based on the restored text, tr. Mark Harman (New York: Schocken, 1998)

The Diaries, tr. Joseph Kresh (New York: Schocken, 1947)

Letters to Friends, Family and Editors, tr. Richard and Clara Winston (New York: Schocken, 1988)

Letters to Felice, tr. James Stern and Elizabeth Duckworth (London: Vintage, 1992)

Letters to Milena, tr. Philip Boehm (New York: Schocken, 1990)

Letters to Ottla and the Family, tr. Richard and Clara Winston (New York: Schocken, 1988)

FURTHER READING

·

The following critical collections provide good introductions:

Julian Preece (ed.), *The Cambridge Companion to Kafka* (Cambridge: Cambridge University Press, 2002)

James Rolleston (ed.), *A Companion to the Works of Franz Kafka* (Rochester, NY: Camden House, 2002)

W. J. Dodd (ed.), *Kafka: The Metamorphosis, The Trial and The Castle, Modern Literatures in Perspective* (London: Longman, 1995)

Mark Anderson (ed.), *Reading Kafka: Prague, Politics, and the Fin de Siècle* (New York: Schocken, 1989)

CHAPTER 1

For biographies of Kafka, see Ronald Hayman, *K: A Biography of Kafka* (London: Weidenfeld and Nicolson, 1980); Ernst Pawel, *The Nightmare of Reason: A Life of Franz Kafka* (London: Harvill, 1984); Nicholas Murray, *Franz Kafka* (London: Little, Brown, 2004); and the small pictorial biography by Jeremy Adler, *Franz Kafka* (London: Penguin, 2001). Reiner Stach is writing a biography in three volumes, the first of which appears in a translation by Shelley Frisch (New York, 2004). For one reasonably rewarding psychoanalytic approach, see Calvin R. Hall and Richard S. Lind, *Dreams, Life and Literature: A Study of Franz Kafka* (Chapel Hill, NC: University of South Carolina Press, 1970).

On Milena Jesenská, see Mary Hockaday, *Kafka, Love and Courage: The Life of Milena Jesenská* (London: Deutsch, 1995); on Dora Diamant, see Kathi Diamant, *Kafka's Last Love: The Mystery of Dora Diamant* (London: Secker and Warburg, 2003). On the question of homosexuality, see Mark Anderson, "Kafka, homosexuality and the aesthetics of 'male culture,'" *Austrian Studies*, 7 (1996), pp. 79–99.

On Kafka's literary setting, see Scott Spector, *Prague Territories: National Conflict and Cultural Innovation in Franz Kafka's Fin de Siècle* (Berkeley, Los Angeles, London: University of California Press, 2000). Intertextual studies include Mark Spilka, *Dickens and Kafka* (Bloomington: Indiana University Press, 1963), and W. J. Dodd, *Kafka and Dostoyevsky: The Shaping of Influence* (London: Macmillan, 1992). On Kafka's travel reading, see John Zilcosky, *Kafka's Travels* (Basingstoke: Palgrave Macmillan, 2003), and on his filmgoing, Hanns Zischler, *Kafka Goes to the Movies* (Chicago and London: University of Chicago Press, 2003). On his publishing career, see Joachim Unseld, *Franz Kafka: A Writer's Life*, tr. Paul F. Dvorak (Riverside, CA: Ariadne Press, 1997).

CHAPTER 2

The distinction formulated by Roland Barthes in *Writing Degree Zero*, tr. Annette Lavers and Colin Smith (London: Cape, 1967) was discussed and developed by Jonathan Culler, *Structuralist Poetics* (London: Routledge and Kegan Paul, 1975). Vladimir Nabokov puzzled over Kafka's entomology in his *Lectures on Literature*, ed. Fredson Bowers (New York: Harcourt Brace Jovanovich, 1980). For Kafka's knowledge of Darwinism and other matters, see Leena Eilittä, *Approaches to Personal Identity in Kafka's Short Fiction: Freud, Darwin, Kierkegaard* (Helsinki: Academia Scientiarum Fennica, 1999).

On Kafka's writing, see Mark Harman's article on his revision of *The Castle* in Rolleston's *Companion* (above), and Malcolm Pasley, "Kafka's *Der Process*: what the manuscript can tell us," *Oxford German Studies*, 18/19 (1989–90), pp. 109–18.

CHAPTER 3

On theories and histories of the body, see Bryan S. Turner, *The Body and Society: Explorations in Social Theory*, 2nd ed. (London: Sage, 1996); Sarah Coakley (ed.), *Religion and the Body* (Cambridge: Cambridge University Press, 1997); Peter Brown, *The Body and Society: Men, Women and Sexual Renunciation in Early Christianity* (New York: Columbia University Press, 1988); E. M. Collingham, *Imperial Bodies: The Physical Experience of the Raj c. 1800–1947* (Cambridge: Polity, 2001). On the body in Kafka's culture, see George L. Mosse, *Nationalism and Sexuality: Respectability and Abnormal Sexuality in Modern Europe* (New York: Fertig, 1985); Mark Anderson, *Kafka's Clothes: Ornament and Aestheticism in the Habsburg Fin de Siècle* (Oxford: Clarendon Press, 1992).

On fasting, see Walter Vandereycken and Ron van Deth, *From Fasting Saints to Anorexic Girls: The History of Self-Starvation* (London: Athlone Press, 1994). On the wound in "A Country Doctor," see especially Edward Timms, "Kafka's expanded metaphors: a Freudian approach to 'Ein Landarzt,'" in J. P. Stern and J. J. White (eds.), *Paths and Labyrinths: Nine Papers from a Kafka Symposium* (London: Institute of Germanic Studies, 1985), pp. 66–79. Erich Heller's essay

"The World of Franz Kafka" is available in his *The Disinherited Mind: Essays in Modern German Literature and Thought* (Cambridge: Bowes and Bowes, 1951).

CHAPTER 4

I have drawn on Erving Goffman, *Asylums* (New York: Doubleday, 1961); Michel Foucault, *Discipline and Punish*, tr. Alan Sheridan (London: Allen Lane, 1977); and Louis Althusser, "Ideology and Ideological State Apparatuses" in *Lenin and Philosophy and Other Essays*, tr. Ben Brewster (London: New Left Books, 1971), pp. 121–73.

Walter Benjamin's famous essay, "Franz Kafka: On the Tenth Anniversary of His Death," is in his *Illuminations*, tr. Harry Zohn (New York: Harcourt, Brace and World, 1968).

For Otto Gross, see Jennifer Michaels, *Anarchy and Eros: Otto Gross' Impact on German Expressionist Writers* (New York: Lang, 1983). The best account of Kafka and law is in Theodore Ziolkowski, *The Mirror of Justice: Literary Reflections of Legal Crises* (Princeton: Princeton University Press, 1997).

The most detailed studies of the rights and wrongs of Kafka's two best-known novels are: Eric L. Marson, *Kafka's Trial: The Case Against Josef K.* (St Lucia: University of Queensland Press, 1975); and Richard Sheppard, *On Kafka's Castle* (London: Croom Helm, 1973), now supplemented by Stephen D. Dowden, *Kafka's Castle and the Critical Imagination* (Columbia, SC: Camden House, 1995).

Johan Huizinga is quoted from his *The Waning of the Middle Ages*, tr. F. Hopman (London: Arnold, 1924). On public executions, see Richard J. Evans, *Rituals of Retribution: Capital Punishment in Germany, 1600–1987* (Oxford: Clarendon Press, 1996).

On Kafka's far-flung family, see Anthony Northey, *Kafka's Relatives: Their Lives and His Writing* (New Haven and London: Yale University Press, 1991); on colonialism, Paul Peters, "Witness to the execution: Kafka and colonialism," *Monatshefte*, 93 (2001), pp. 401–25; on minor literatures, Gilles Deleuze and Félix Guattari, *Kafka: Toward a Minor Literature*, tr. Dana Polan (Minneapolis: University of Minnesota Press, 1986).

For a thorough feminist reading, consult Elizabeth Boa, *Kafka: Gender, Class and Race in the Letters and Fictions* (Oxford: Clarendon Press, 1996).

CHAPTER 5

On Kafka and Judaism, see Evelyn Torton Beck, *Kafka and the Yiddish Theater* (Madison, WI: Wisconsin University Press, 1971); Ritchie Robertson, *Kafka: Judaism, Politics, and Literature* (Oxford: Clarendon Press, 1985). See the discussion of Kafka in *The Correspondence of Walter Benjamin and Gershom Scholem, 1932–1940*, tr. Gary Smith and Andre Lefevere (New York: Schocken, 1989). On Kafka and Kierkegaard, see Richard Sheppard, "Kafka, Kierkegaard and the K.s: theology, psychology and fiction," *Journal of Literature and Theology*, 5 (1991), pp. 277–96. As background, see William James, *The Varieties of Religious Experience* (London and New York: Longmans, Green and Co., 1902).

INDEX

•

Page numbers in *italics* include illustrations and photographs/captions.

PICTURE CREDITS

•

ART RESOURCE: 7, 121: Snark/Art Resource, NY. **BRIDGEMAN ART LIBRARY**: 63.
CORBIS: 14, 21, 97: © Bettmann/CORBIS; 94: © Simon Mein/Sygma/CORBIS; 123:
© Hulton-Deutsch Collection/CORBIS; 137: © David Rubinger/CORBIS; 146: ©
Jeremy Horner/CORBIS. **GETTY**: viii: Getty Images. **LEBRECHT PHOTO LIBRARY**:
3, 15: Leemage/Lebrecht Music & Arts; 26, 92: Interfoto/Lebrecht Music & Arts
COURTESY OF THE NATIONAL LIBRARY OF MEDICINE: 54. **COURTESY
OF THE NEW YORK TIMES**: 69. **COURTESY OF PRINTS & PHOTOGRAPHS
DIVISION, LIBRARY OF CONGRESS**: 23: LC-USZ62-120920; 29: LC-USZ62-99147;
49: LC-USZ62-49911; 80: LC-USZ62-68568; 85: LC-USZ62-71678; 102: LC-USZ62-
74580; 107: LC-USZ62-116133; 111: LC-USZ62-49880; 115: LC-DIG-ppmsca-00394;
116: LC-DIG-pga-01879; 118: LC-DIG-nclc-04523; 120: LC-DIG-ppmsc-09214; 126:
LC-DIG-ppmsc-09996; 132–33: LC-USZ62-108469; 135t: LC-DIG-ppmsc-07261;
135b: LC-DIG-ppmsc-09290; 140: LC-DIG-ppmsca-18675. **COURTESY OF
WIKIMEDIA COMMONS**: ii: Franz Kafka in 1906; 19: Franz Grillparzer/Upload by
Andreas Praefcke; 20: Gustave Flaubert/Upload by Patche99z; 36: *Tower of Blue Horses*
by Franz Marc/Yorck Project: 10.000 Meisterwerke der Malerei; 37: *Die Verwandlung*
(*The Transformation*)/Upload by H.-P.Haack; 41t: Ernst Haeckel ca. 1918; 41b: Friedrich
Nietzsche ca. 1875; 43: The killing of Cleitus by Andre Castaigne; 58: *Der Zauberberg*
(*The Magic Mountain*)/Upload by H.-P.Haack; 77: Page from Codex Tchacos/Upload
by WolfgangRieger; 78: *St. Jerome* by Albrecht Altdorfer/Yorck Project: 10.000 Meisterwerke der Malerei; 105: Fettmilch Riot; 141: *Søren Kierkegaard at His High Desk* by
Luplau Janssen; 143: Sigmund Freud in 1926; 149: Moses and the burning bush/Upload
by Vassil

BRIEF INSIGHTS

•

A series of concise, engrossing, and enlightening books that explore every subject under the sun with unique insight.

Available now or coming soon: